RIDING
FOR THE
BLUE

A Celebration
of Horse Shows

RIDING
FOR THE
BLUE

A Celebration
of Horse Shows

By Cindy Hale

Photographs by
Sharon P. Fibelkorn

A Division of Fancy Publications
Irvine, California

Ruth Strother, Project Manager
Nick Clemente, Special Consultant
Karla Austin, Editor
Michelle Martinez, Assistant Editor
Cover and book design by Bocu & Bocu

Library of Congress Cataloging-in-Publication Data
Hale, Cindy.
  Riding for the blue : a celebration of horse shows / by Cindy Hale ;
photographs by Sharon P. Fibelkorn.
     p. cm.
  ISBN 1-931993-06-8 (hardback : alk. paper)
  1. Horse shows. 2. Horses--Showing. 3. Show riding. I. Fibelkorn,
Sharon P. II. Title.
  SF294.5 .H35 2003
  798.2'4--dc21

                           2002011099

BowTie™ Press
A Division of Fancy Publications
3 Burroughs
Irvine, California 92618

Printed and Bound in Singapore
10 9 8 7 6 5 4 3 2 1

For my mother, who will always be "Queen of the Horse Show Moms" — CH

ACKNOWLEDGMENTS

Riding for the Blue

could not have been completed without the support of
competitors, judges, trainers, and all the other horse lovers
who populate the show scene. In many instances, those who
contributed personal anecdotes are named within the book.
Others offered their expertise to help me gain background
information—they remain anonymous, but their help in
this endeavor is duly noted with much thanks.

On the professional front, Moira C. Harris,
the editor of Horse Illustrated *magazine, served as*
head cheerleader and impromptu mental health counselor.
The fact that she could do her own job, hold my hand,
and still find time to ride her horse is testament to her
personal fortitude and character.

CONTENTS

Preface

HORSE SHOWS IN THE SUN

INDIO, CALIFORNIA

HITS
INDIO
DESERT

I REMEMBER MY FIRST BLUE RIBBON.

I was a scrawny, insecure little girl dressed in hand-me-down show apparel perched aboard my scruffy, flame-colored pony Honeybee. That particular show was tiny and so was the blue ribbon, but the exhilarating feeling I got, believing at that instant all eyes of the universe were upon me in my moment of glory, had me hooked. Now, after more than thirty years of equestrian competition, I can honestly say that I've never seen a blue ribbon I didn't want.

I'm fortunate that I'm able to combine my love for horses and showing with my writing career. In that regard, my sincere wish is for *Riding for the Blue* to serve three purposes. First, it is my attempt to convey the appeal of horse shows to nonequestrians. Even my husband cannot make the connection between my euphoria over a piece of blue satin and my months of struggling to get my mare to jump quietly around a hunter course. My second goal is to have other competitive riders, regardless of their chosen discipline or skill level, look at this book and sigh, *Ah, yes, that is what my life's passion is about.* Both Sharon Fibelkorn and I strove to capture, through images and text, the unifying themes of all horse shows: the spirit of sportsmanship, the camaraderie of friends, and a rider's bond with her horse. Finally, and for me most important, *Riding for the Blue* is a love letter sent to the horse show world with a note of thanks for what the many years of participation has taught me. I am no doubt a better person for what I've learned about myself as a competitor and as a companion to my horses.

Cindy Hale

CALIFORNIA
SADDLE
HORSE
FUTURITY
HORSE
SHOW

POMONA,
CALIFORNIA
2001

CHAMPION

Chapter 1

LET'S SHOW!

WHAT IGNITES THE COMPETITIVE SPARK?

Does it happen the first time a lead liner finally masters the up/down of the posting trot? The moment a western rider discovers just the right pace for a lope? And what continues to lure the seasoned exhibitor? Surely she has better things to do on a weekend than rise before dawn and shimmy into uncomfortable body-hugging, restrictive attire and spend the day hiking back and forth from horse trailer to show arena. If this ceaseless activity, usually occurring in the extremes of either dust-choking air or sloppy mud, doesn't discourage her, the food offered at the concession stands will. This unrelenting schedule, which likely includes second-guessing the whimsies of judges, would grate against the soul of most anyone. Yet riders still continue to line up at entry booths in that unending quest for blue ribbons and moments of notoriety. Undoubtedly, the motivating factor is a passionate love for horses. Each dedicated equestrian has taken an unspoken vow of allegiance to her horse, a commitment to honor the bond that exists between horse and rider. This is as it should be, for in no other sport is a human required to communicate with an animal to such a degree. A mere pair of reins, the touch of a boot's heel, and the chirp of a "cluck" are virtually the only tools allowed as human and equine compete as a team.

A horse, being an animal with a feral ancestry, often gives in to instinctual urges even when domesticated. The most highly trained show horse can resort to fractious behavior in unfamiliar settings. The show ring is a scary place for a horse until he accepts his rider as his leader: jumps look suspicious, the water truck monstrous, and the voice of the announcer threatening. When a 1,200-pound horse entrusts his safety to a human and performs reliably in the show ring, it's a heady accomplishment. The blue ribbon is merely the tangible reward. Of course, it's also an added bonus when that same champion horse is the rider's best friend. The jumper who digs his heels into the turf to clear that final oxer, the pony who is the only steed who doesn't spook when the dust devil blows through the arena, and the dressage horse who adds a touch of panache to his tempi changes, all endear themselves further to their riders. When these same horses slurp a cola, ham it up for their win photos, or snack on the show ring's decorative flora, it makes them even more priceless.

Yet a strong bond between a rider and her horse isn't enough. To be successful, a rider must possess a thick skin because rejection comes swift and hard. Despite hours of preparation, one missed lead or a chip at one jump can send her back to the trailer with no hope of a ribbon. She must also be armed with a take-no-prisoners approach to competing. She has to look her fellow riders in the eye

and think to herself, *My horse and I are the best today, and now I'll show you why.* Junior riders are the experts at this tactic, particularly those in medal and horsemanship events. You can see them in the horse show office, studying the posted class list, weighing their competitors' merits with the calculating eyes of a military strategist. These are the same teens who earlier had cavorted in the host motel's pool with their rivals or shared a helping of nachos with their nemesis at the food booth. But now, twenty minutes before the class is called to order, it's war.

The adult amateur riders, mostly women, take a different approach to showing. Two lady friends, still in their show clothes, can chat like teenagers at the back gate for hours. The topics? Dishing horse show gossip is the usual but so is anything remotely horsey. At home, they're limited to how much they can ramble on about chaps, velveteen helmets, and the benefits of aluminum horseshoes. But

here, they can talk unrestrained about such topics. Though the sun may make them squint, forming little crow's feet at the edges of their eyes, they don't care. After all, it's a horse show, and they're among friends. Who's going to chide them if there's boot polish underneath their fingernails?

Amidst the competition, the kaleidoscope of color among horses and riders shines: the preppy fashion coda of khaki and navy in the hunt-seat world versus the jewel-toned chaps and spandex body suits of the western classes. Silver ponies with charcoal muzzles stand rump-to-rump with chestnuts who shine like copper coins and shiny satin ribbons contrast with the matte finish of buffed leather. And everywhere there is noise, from the crackling of the public announcement system (do any of them ever work properly?) to the slosh of arena sand against the backside of a jump. The sights and sounds only add to the emotional tension as riders and horses wait to compete against their peers and aim for the perfect performance.

"Horse shows can take you from the depths of despair to the heights of ecstasy—and that's just on warm-up day," says Emily Caldon, an adult amateur hunt-seat rider. "I've had some of my worst rounds in front of huge crowds and felt like slinking away. But I've also had horses suddenly rise to the occasion and put in a great trip when they've been awful at home, and it's like a miraculous victory." The emotional roller coaster, however, doesn't deter her. "To me, riding is a sport, not a hobby. I welcome the challenges of competing. What's the point of practicing so hard if you're not even going to the game?"

"It's like no other feeling in the world," says Tom Sworm, an American saddlebred trainer and horse show judge. "When you're showing a saddlebred that's really firing off all four legs, that loves competing and knows its job, you just put it in gear and stay out of its way. It's like driving a well-tuned Ferrari."

Dressage rider Debbie McDonald is a United States champion and Pan Am Games gold medal winner. Her motivation to show is built upon an undeniable bond with her mounts. "Horses are my friends.

They're the reason I get up every morning," says McDonald. Despite the pressures of international competition, she thrives in the sport because "it's an adrenaline rush you can't find in any other atmosphere."

Fifty-nine-year-old Marty Shaughnessy still competes with his Appaloosa in reining and heritage-costume events. He sees a sense of pride and accomplishment in his blue ribbons. "I can say to myself, when I win at the Appaloosa world show, that at that moment in time, I'm the best in the world in that event."

Sarah Wilson, a young rider who competes in a variety of events, mostly at 4-H shows, sums up the appeal of horse shows as perhaps only an eleven-year-old could. "I like showing. I get to see my friends, and even though we're riding against each other, we cheer each other on. Yeah, we're competing. But it's all in fun."

Unfortunately, such fun comes at a price. While there are shows that serve the skill level of every rider, from backyard offerings at a local riding school to weeklong extravaganzas with national media coverage, they all stretch the pocketbook. Nearly everyone has to find creative ways to indulge their passion for competing. Before venturing into the realm of competition, there are two rules of showing that every exhibitor needs to memorize:

Rule Number One: Showing is an expensive endeavor. In the hypothetical pie chart of expenses, the cost of the horse accounts for just a medium-sized slice of pie. It's out-sliced by entry fees, motel fees, overnight stabling fees, fees to join the local riding association that sanctions the show, coaching fees, grooming fees, and trailering fees. And then there's another slice of the pie chart for all the "stuff." Yes, a rider must have stuff to compete. There are show trunks, show tack, show clothes, and horsey accessories just for shows. And just when the rider is sick

of eating pie, guess what? Fashion trends change, fads disappear, and it becomes imperative to dispense of all the old stuff and buy all new stuff—all of which ties into...

Rule Number Two: The amount of money spent is inversely proportional to the amount of fun enjoyed. This is also known as The Equestrian's Law of Painful Irony. A rider's plans for a dream show, the event she budgeted for six months in advance forcing her to eat macaroni and cheese three nights a week, will be the very same show in which her horse spies a ghost in the far corner of the arena or breaks out in hives from the bedding in the show stall.

By keeping these two simple rules in mind, a rider will prevent herself from ever contemplating the validity of her relatives' notion that she has become certifiably insane ever since she entered her first horse show. Now she realizes what she's gotten herself into: a most glorious way in which to spend oodles of money while enjoying the companionship of good friends, the loyalty of a spirited horse, and the challenge of competition. So, let's show!

Chapter 2

THE HUNT FOR ELEGANCE

FOR THOSE HORSE SHOW OBSERVERS WHO

can't quite comprehend the whole point of the hunter division, here's a statement that sums up the objective of the competition: It's supposed to look easy.

A 16-plus-hand horse, usually controlled by nothing more than a simple snaffle bit, is guided around a course of eight jumps. Each takeoff must be precise, or the rhythmic flow of the round is disrupted and the horse's style suffers. Too close of a takeoff and the horse is apt to hang a leg or twist his body in an awkward effort. Leave from too far back and the arc is flat. In this event, the horse more resembles a hare diving for his burrow. Between the jumps the horse must gallop with low, ground-covering strides. He mustn't be arguing with his rider, either. At each corner, if necessary, he must nonchalantly perform a flying lead change.

The rider, for the most part, serves merely as navigator. She aims the horse toward each successive jump and regulates the speedometer, but for the most part, the horse does all the work. Too much obvious riding and the flow of the round suffers. There are really only two skills a hunter rider needs to bring to the arena: a dependable eye for negotiating a takeoff and the willingness to stay the heck out of the way of a good horse's performance.

The hunter division descends from the British and East Coast American tradition of foxhunting. Why are the manes of hunters at nationally rated shows braided? Because foxhunters braided their horses' manes to keep them free of brambles and twigs. What is the significance of a show ring hunter who exudes good manners and a submissive attitude? During a cross-country foxhunt, amid a herd of galloping horses, a frolicking horse could incite a melee. Why are the clothes of the hunter  rider so formal? Who decided that the best outfit for perching on the back of a jumping horse was a suit blazer, a long-sleeved, starched cotton shirt, and a pair of breeches with as much elasticity as cardboard? Thank the classic traditions of the foxhunt. Keep a stiff upper lip, my dear. Yes, your velvet hunt cap is giving you a migraine, but by golly you look smashing!

There is an undeniable aesthetic beauty to the hunter division. The quietly elegant accessories accent the attributes—rhythm and style—of a winning round. The well-oiled tack is the color of oak bark and mahogany. There's a hint of sparkle in the stainless steel bits and stirrup irons and in the dollop of brass found on bridle nametags, but nowhere is there a whisper of gaudiness. The clothes are demure. Navy blue hunt coats are standard issue, though the palette threatens to expand into the browns and grays. A female rider can flirt with fashion by wearing a shirt in lemon yellow or lavender, but appearing coy by wearing lots of makeup or snazzy jewelry is cause for dismissal from the corps. Class is not ostentatious.

Since the hunter division sprang from the leisure time activities of the moneyed horsey set, it's only fitting that, especially at the upper levels of competition, the quality of the horse begins to reflect the cash flow activities of their owners. For the most part, the show hunters found at the back gate of an A-rated show are a divinely inspired contingency of gorgeous animals, from their chiseled profiles to their long hips and sloping shoulders. Each one skims the ground at the trot, pointing his toes like a ballet artist, cantering to the jumps almost in slow motion, pausing at the moment of takeoff to rock back on rippling haunches and then spring up and over the jump in a single motion that lifts knees to chin. The best hunters jump with such roundness to their form that they nearly toss their riders out of the saddle.

The majority of these horses are bred to be show hunters. Whether Thoroughbred or warmblood, their pedigree is rich with relatives who jumped for a living. But occasionally one is discovered after he's discarded from an earlier career at the racetrack or plucked as a youngster from the backyard of a naïve breeder. There is great rejoicing at such a find, when talent is revealed in the guise of a humble, rough-coated colt. The prospect of finding the proverbial diamond in the rough is what lures English riders of modest income to haunt the auctions, the racetrack, and the small farms for their ticket to the major shows. With training and polish, the talented horse can pass muster with his blue-blooded rivals. Then even the country folk can ride for a blue ribbon.

The best hunter I ever showed was my sister's gelding Baba Yaga. He was a quarter horse, but at 17.2 hands with long legs and a sweet face, he easily masqueraded as a Thoroughbred. No one was the wiser with regard to him spending most weekdays bopping down trails in a western saddle. But in the show ring, he was all business. With his huge stride he could cruise down the lines on a soft rein and then snap his knees into a tight bundle over the jumps. As a hunter, his only fault was that he wasn't a very good mover. He had a tad too much animation to his canter. My trainer Bob would always tell me, "Win the class on the jumps. Be consistent. You be perfect, and let the other riders make mistakes." I swear sometimes Baba Yaga would twist his big bay head back at me and echo the same instructions with an added, *Yeah, dummy*.

The horse knew his job. If I made an error, particularly if I bumped him with my heel over the top of an oxer, I'd pay for it when his front hooves hit the ground. More than once he pitched me off. Usually I was unaware that I'd offended the horse until I'd hear either Bob or my sister take a ragged breath and sigh, "Uh-oh." Then I had about two seconds to pick up the contact on my reins and deepen my heels. But the horse was a champ, often earning enough prize money to pay for an entire week of show expenses. More important, he taught me how to ride.

Rick and Buffy Oas have a similar fondness for their mare, Wait n' See, affectionately nicknamed Rosie. They discovered her when she was a gangly, rough-coated four-year-old, yet they could see beyond the ragged coat and the lack of weight. As Buffy recalled, "Her knees were so close together that they touched." But when they enlisted the help of a nearby dressage rider to climb aboard for a test drive, they were encouraged. The young horse revealed a willing disposition and an uncanny jumping ability. The husband and wife team liked what they saw and bought the filly.

Like most horses with warmblood bloodlines, Rosie took her time maturing. "It took a year and a half for her to learn her flying lead changes," says Buffy. "All of our hunters do dressage, and the dressage work is what helped Rosie get her changes." It was literally a game of wait-and-see until Rosie reached her full potential. Eventually she began capturing major wins at A-rated shows. Four years after she was plucked from obscurity, Rick rode her to the amateur owner championship (for riders eighteen to thirty-five years old) at the National Hunter/Jumper Council's 2001 National Finals.

As for the mare's current status as one of America's leading show hunters, Buffy describes the mare as a princess. "She loves to show off, and she knows she's being watched," reveals Buffy. "I tell my friends that, yes, my husband has a girlfriend: Her name is Rosie. Oh, yeah, and she has four legs." Needless to say, the mare's personality, plus her winning ways, makes her a recipient of much devotion.

Chapter 3

THE WESTERN MYSTIQUE

IT'S UNDERSTANDABLE THAT IN OUR TECHNO-DEPENDENT, asphalt-and-stucco society, the allure of the western lifestyle remains strong, with its pure-hearted cowboys who are kind to their horses and loyal to their women. The romance of the West is distinctly American and proudly represents a large division of classes at American horse shows. Adherence to the cult compels many average Americans who don't spend much time in the saddle to squiggle into Wrangler jeans, listen to country music, and buy a pickup truck (complete with trailer hitch). Just look at contemporary home décor: an entire genre of interior decorating has been formulated upon the notion that a lariat can substitute for a front door wreath, and a pile of discarded horse shoes can be welded into patio furniture. A stroll among the western-styled participants at a horse show reveals a panacea for world-weary senses. There is the creak of thick leather as a rider slings herself into her saddle. The patina of engraved silver conchos buffed by years of rough-out chaps and buttery deerskin gloves shimmers softly in the afternoon light. Patterns abound, from the tobiano patches to the geometric weavings of a Navajo saddle blanket. Touch the hand-braided reins of a hackamore: they're rough and prickly. Nearly everyone wears spurs with rowels. And they really do jingle-jangle with each step. This is no place for the preppy navy-and-tan riding uniforms of the hunt-seat set or for fancy haberdashery. Forget the monograms and the pearl stud earrings—the mood here is authentic, the real deal. While few Americans have ever ridden on a foxhunt, they're all familiar with the cowboy culture. Even if the real cowboys and cowgirls are back home tending the ranch, at least their fans can commune for a weekend of western mystique.

To distinguish themselves from their English counterparts, the western exhibitors have concocted their own horse show lingo. The arena is referred to as a pen, which seems more fitting since that is where livestock are corralled on a ranch. The horses don't trot and canter, they jog and lope. Just the two terms themselves conjure up images of a horse and rider ambling down a trail hemmed by sagebrush. "I'm going to lope on over to the north forty," sounds much more bucolic than, "I shall canter after the hounds." English saddles are secured with a girth, western stock saddles with a cinch—one sounds restrictive, the other laidback and simple. Rawhide, latigo, romal, riata: The jargon of the western rider is part Spanish, part Texas, part riding off into the sunset.

If the cowboy symbolizes the heritage of the American West, it is the cowgirl who symbolizes style and pizzazz on the show circuit. Male competitors are relegated to the standard issue western attire, meaning they wear the same long-sleeved shirts and boot-cut slacks that most chief executive officers (CEOs) west of the Mississippi do every Saturday. But oh, those ladies! They're expected to clothe themselves in spangled duds to make the fellows and the judges sit up on their pockets and take notice. From slinky mock turtleneck leotard tops to bosom-hugging vests trimmed in sequins, the overtly feminine aspects of ladies' western show attire is a flirtatious mix of eye appeal and sex appeal. Want to wear makeup? Don't forget the lipstick. Like the look of silver concho earrings? Buy the matching necklace, too.

"All horse shows are theater," says Suzi Drnec, the president of Hobby Horse Clothing, Inc., a leading manufacturer of customized western show apparel. "The riders are the actors on stage and the judge is the audience. Anything vaguely western is like our national costume. It brings pride and uniqueness to the wearer. Western show riders just constantly reinterpret the classic elements of silver, denim, and leather," says Drnec. When selecting their wardrobe, the western ladies mustn't neglect coordinating the color of their ensemble with that of their horse. To that end, the Hobby Horse catalog provides a color wheel. Scarlet goes with dark bay, emerald with sorrel, and citrus with palomino.

Many breeds of horses compete in western events, including Arabians, Appaloosas, and saddlebreds. Nearly every equestrian enthusiast has an opportunity to "cowboy up" for the judge. But the heart and soul of the entire western division belongs to the quarter horse. Even the paint, who is primarily a quarter horse that spent too much time at the cosmetic counter, doesn't rival the quarter horse's popularity. This seems only fitting, since the quarter horse is revered as America's horse, having been developed during Colonial times by crossing scrappy local horses with bloodline, aristocratic equines imported from Europe. The result was a supremely versatile, even-tempered utilitarian horse with a knack for besting Thoroughbreds in sprint races. As the colonists expanded west, the quarter horse's gift for short bursts of speed was invaluable in securing wayward calves. As the breed was refined, and the sport of equestrian competition grew, the quarter horse not only found a home on the range but also in the show ring.

Renowned quarter horse breeder, trainer, and judge Lynn Palm cited the infusion of Thoroughbred blood into the modern quarter horse's lineage as the change that helped make the breed the versatile horse it is today. "It's made it the most successful horse in competition. Today's quarter horse can do all the English disciplines from dressage to hunters and driving, yet still be very competitive for trail and western riding," says Palm. Adding to the quarter horse's appeal is his dependable disposition. Because of his trademark docile temperament "a lot of people can participate in riding," says Palm. "The horse can tolerate a great deal. You can work the ranch on it all day long." Yet while he's still the supreme choice for cattle work, there's no denying that the quarter horse in today's show ring is a far cry from the small, sturdy cayuse with the bulldog build. Nope. He's certainly not your grandfather's quarter horse.

Few events showcase the quarter horse's natural talent more than the reined cow horse class, and nowhere else is the western mystique more personified. The romance of the West is distilled down to its basic elements: a cowboy and his trusty quarter horse alternately sweet-talking and commandeering a steer into submission. Each horse is first tested for his obedience and agility as he performs a structured pattern, referred to as dry work. Large figure eights are galloped, demonstrating smooth flying lead changes with nary a visible cue from the rider. The horse must also spin on his haunches and slide to a stop. Both are maneuvers that if done well elicit whoops of approval from spectators.

If the dry work is indicative of the horse's skill, the cow work reveals the horse's true mettle. A gate opens and a steer is prodded into the pen. The judge watches, discerning whether or not the horse possesses that innate trademark of the quarter horse—the ability to read the mind of the steer, to outthink and outwit the bovine who so desperately wants to rejoin his herd. Does the horse lock up with the steer? Does he defy the steer to make a break for freedom? As he dances with the steer, shod hoof against cloven hoof, he takes on the aspects of a cheetah: a slinking, low-slung center of gravity with so much sinewy muscle, so much predatory instinct.

At a signal from the judge's booth, the battle escalates. Now the rail work begins, as the rider tells the horse just how to master the steer, how to commandeer him, how to force him to circle, how to turn him along the fence line. For some horses, it's a game of tag. They seem to almost tease the steer, *Think you can make it past me? Go ahead. Give it a shot.* The more aggressive horses view it as a wrestling match, where strategy combines with brawn in an attempt to overcome the opponent. Ears are pinned on both combatants. Body language threatens violence, but neither animal has the time to make good on the warnings. Every second can earn points from the judge, and the veteran horses seem to sense the clock is ticking. Their family name is on the line. Another bell sounds and the duel is over. The rider lifts the reins, and the horse complies, stretching his neck, damp with sweat, down to the bit. With a well-earned pat, he settles back into his role as the cowboy's sidekick.

Chapter 4

Dressage—Harmony on Horseback

IT IS PERHAPS EASIER TO EXPLAIN THE BEAUTY

and allure of dressage by defining what it is not. Dressage is not mind-numbing, pointless flatwork. It is not an equestrian sport reserved only for dowagers, aristocrats, or heiresses. The horses themselves need not be imported warmbloods christened with unpronounceable names. To say dressage resembles "a horse and rider dancing together" is not only a threadbare cliché but it's also not entirely correct. In its purest form, dressage is an avenue for all riders to achieve a harmonious relationship with their horses.

In dressage, the rider and the horse must function as a team: the rider is the captain and the horse is the most valuable player. The horse, blessed with a benevolent demeanor and a generous attitude, acquiesces, responding to the slightest of aids: every movement of the rider's hands and every ounce of pressure exerted by the seat or legs mean something to the trained dressage horse. Yet the horse is never dominated; he remains an enthusiastic team member. To ensure such willing compliance, the dressage horse is brought along slowly. There is such meticulous attention to detail during the horse's training that an outsider might get the notion that the dressage rider is suffering from an equine-induced fugue of obsessive compulsiveness.

A foundation is built upon training basics. As those rudimentary skills are mastered, the next level of skills is introduced. Some horses, perhaps taxed by the inauspicious talents of their rider or vexed by poor conformation, never rise above the lower levels. But those animals gifted with good genes, good training, and a good mind become the epitome of dressage. Even the uninitiated horse person, untainted by bradoons, piaffes, and shadbellies, can appreciate the lofty gaits and precision timing of a Grand Prix test.

Dressage shows are run quite differently from other competitions and seem ensconced in an educational theme. Perhaps in an effort to curtail too much recess time, show managers give each competitor a specific time to report to class. Horses and riders don't perform over a course; they ride a test. The tests are standard prescribed exams detailed in a primer, which all dressage riders learn by rote—it is akin to learning the ABCs. In fact, the dressage ring (called a court) is lined with imposing blocks of capital letters, which are markers that signal when each transition should take place. Lower level riders who aren't quick studies are permitted readers who stand outside the dressage court and dictate aloud the required movements step by regimented step. Riders receive their grades, which are presented in percentage scores based on their performances, each served with a form that includes written comments from the judge. The comments can be either encouraging or stinging, but they are always informative. The judge's critique is usually filled with homework assignments. There are very few A-pluses in dressage.

No equestrian stereotype is lampooned as often as the Dressage Queen (DQ). Rarely is she the battle-tested, accomplished dressage rider whose visage is crisscrossed with crow's feet from staring down the centerline to locate X. No, this throne is reserved for the dilettante—the rider who knows just enough to make her equal parts annoying and fascinating. Her Royal Haughtiness embodies the hoity-toity attitude that more bourgeois riders associate with dressage. For the most part, the association is unfair. But that doesn't mean that the DQ doesn't exist in reality. In fact, she is ubiquitous. A rider will encounter at least one DQ at every dressage competition. Despite her familiarity, she's impossible to ignore. She's a common native bird, yet one so remarkable in plumage that riders find it hard to look away. The DQ's standard attire is a pair of figure-hugging breeches with a full leather seat. Her boots, with spurs affixed to their heels, are always ready—they're stashed in the backseat of her car,

which sports brand decals of six different warmblood registries in the rear windshield. And then there's her voice. Tinged with a continental accent and peppered with Germanic slang, it is purposely just loud enough to be overheard from where she enthralls her retinue directly in line with X, that unmarked no-man's-land that's understood by competitors to be the absolute center of the dressage court. Here she pontificates confidently, detailing the merits—or more likely the demerits—of each test ridden before her gaze. To punctuate her remarks, she waves her three-foot-long, silver-tipped dressage whip like a scepter. Ironically, the DQ is rarely observed competing herself. She is annoying, but she is amusing. Yet the horse show world would be a less colorful milieu without her. Long live the Dressage Queen!

Debbie McDonald is no dressage queen. She grew up with humble roots competing in both western and English classes at small community shows with her chubby bay pony, Flanagan. Later, she spent years as a top hunter and jumper competitor, then moved on to dressage. "I used to think dressage looked so boring—all flatwork, all day long," says McDonald. "I didn't realize how difficult it was." Despite its difficulties, she mastered the art of dressage winning numerous awards: the American Horse Shows Association (AHSA) Equestrian of the Year 2000; the United States Olympic Committee Horsewoman of the Year 2000; the gold medal at the 1999 Pan Am Games; the 2001 United States Grand Prix Dressage Championship; and the 2002 USAEquestrian National Freestyle Championship.

Participation in the Olympics seems likely. Yet all that showing experience still hasn't squelched tinges of performance anxiety before riding at an important competition. "I get very nervous before my tests. But it's not fear. It's more of a feeling of excitement, of anticipation. Once I get on my horse,

though, I'm fine, which is good because in dressage your horse is so tuned to your aids that they can be affected by any nervous tension," says McDonald. "Probably the hardest aspect of dressage competition, especially compared to hunters and jumpers—and I know you get in a 'zone' with them, too—is that in the higher levels of dressage you're doing very advanced movements that are required in a rapid sequence. As a rider, you simply cannot allow your mind to wander, even for a second." What's the payoff for such stress? "There's an incredible feeling of being one with the horse. The two of us are working together with one, unified brain," explains McDonald.

Her efforts are aided by the solid work ethic in Brentina, the 16.2-hand Hanoverian mare she's ridden to so many wins. "She always rises to the occasion," says McDonald. "I like to say she 'puffs up' at shows. It's so true that a dressage horse must not only want to perform, it must enjoy it, too. You know, I'm a small woman so I cannot physically force or muscle my way into making a horse the size of Brentina perform. She's really happy every day she comes out of the stall to work." Brentina, owned by Peggy Thomas, has been paired with McDonald since the mare was a three-year-old. The two have developed a close bond. "We have our own way of communicating," explains McDonald. "I realized a long time ago how dependent horses are on us for their care. Maybe it's a maternal instinct to not only want to take good care of them but I also think that's why I feel so close to my horse. She depends on me, and my heart aches when I think about the time that eventually she won't be with me anymore."

Chapter 5

JUMPERS—GRACE UNDER PRESSURE

THE JUMPER STANDS AT THE INGATE, A LANKY BAY

gelding with a coat the color of fawn and a thick black tail cut blunt at the fetlocks. The horse is outfitted in full regalia, armaments for a battle against the course and the clock: an elastic breastplate to hold the saddle secure; caramel-colored boots to protect the front legs; navy polo wraps for support on the back; a crocheted ear bonnet to seal out annoying gnats atop his head; and a leather belly guard to protect his underside, lest he smack himself with an enthusiastic hoof in midair. His rider is less distinguished in her attire: boots, breeches, a blue knitted shirt, and a black helmet. These are workman-like clothes for the serious athlete—no need for the frills of calfskin gloves or monogrammed haberdashery.

Cued by the sound of the starter, the rider clucks at her horse to send him onto the turf field. She eyes the course one last time, catching a glimpse of a collection of brightly striped poles and panels hung between standards that appear to be crafted by Disney artisans. A pair of enormous turquoise butterflies adorns one set; another jump resembles a cactus garden complete with a rustic wagon wheel. Yet this theme park atmosphere deters neither horse nor rider. Instead, both seem to have a small confab about their strategy as the rider whispers the route once more with a mental notation to make the inside turn to 4A and B. An electronic tone, a metallic gong unlike any other audible signal and unique to the horse show world, sounds. It's time to begin. The horse, conditioned to the significance of the sound, springs into action.

Always looking ahead, always cueing her horse over the top of the jump, always communicating, *Go here, turn now, faster through this part, now wait through this line,* to her mount, her wishes conveyed via reins and a shift of weight in the saddle. The horse, eager to do his rider's bidding and mightily enjoying this game over obstacles, tugs at the bit and pulls the reins taut against the rings of the martingale. When asked to go deep at a vertical, his legs stab the ground like pistons. When sent long to a wide oxer, he stretches out his neck, rolls his shoulders forward and snaps his knees up to his velvet chin. While airborne, he seems suspended for seconds. Every detail of his anatomy is evident: the sinewy muscles, the adrenaline-flushed veins, and the crimson lining of flared nostrils. Even his steel shoes, drilled and tapped, spiked with half-inch studs, flash brightly in the sun. Down the final combination they charge! As they land after the last oxer, the rider touches a spur to her horse's side and asks for a final burst of flat-out speed to blast them through the timers. Above the grandstand, an electronic scoreboard displays the fractions of seconds as they flutter away. Steel caulks tear into the turf and catapult a chunk of sod into the grandstand. Such is the power and speed that symbolizes the world of show jumping.

The jumper division used to be the last stop, the catch basin for horses who didn't move well enough for dressage or who weren't stylish enough for hunters. The rogues were welcomed as were horses cursed with an unfortunate blemish to their conformation. But today, when the Grand Prix circuit offers tens of thousands of dollars in prize money, horses are bred, raised, and nurtured to be specialists in the sport. As unbroken youngsters, naïve about the feel of leather against their skin, they're evaluated for their length of stride, natural balance, innate jumping abilities, and zest for work.

Equally gutsy riders are drawn to a discipline where the judge's taste in horseflesh never comes into play. Rules for competition are rather simplistic: jump cleanly and jump fast. But a rider had better know the rules by rote before venturing into the game. A variety of scoring systems called tables explain in great detail how the blue ribbon can be won. It's purely objective, yet for the show official who must

adjudicate any bizarre happenstance, it can be a disquieting assignment. Jumper judges must study all of the scoring tables, then pass a written exam that proposes all sorts of hypothetical situations. What if a horse hits a rail, but the rail doesn't plunk to the ground until the rider has already passed through the timers? What if an overexuberant rider makes a turn that loops back across her own tracks? What if a rider notices her saddle is in a precarious position and dismounts to readjust it after she's been signaled to begin on course? Suddenly, the jumper judge,

who's been dutifully checking boxes on his scorecard and merely jotting down the faults and time on course, must come to attention. "I'd compare judging jumpers to flying an airplane," quips jumper official Robert McDonald. "It's hours of boredom punctuated with moments of sheer panic."

Molly Ashe began her competitive career as a precocious five-year-old. She remembers riding her pony in the short stirrup classes at the famous Harrisburg, Pennsylvania, horse shows. Her junior years culminated in her being one of the most accomplished riders of her generation. Later, she took time off for college and to reevaluate her options in the show world. She decided not to return to the hunter arena but to pursue show jumping—and she's done so in a big way. Winning multiple Grand Prix competitions and being named to the United States Equestrian Team's (USET) developing rider's program, she has proved her skill as a jumper. As a prediction of where her talent will take her, she piloted Sandra O'Donnell's Dutch warmblood mare, Kroon Gravin, to the American Grand Prix Association's Horse of the Year title in 2000. In 2002, Ashe and Kroon Gravin were selected as members of the USETs show jumping squad for the World Equestrian Games. This accolade came after the two went through six grueling rounds of trials in which they accrued the fewest cumulative faults.

In a sport where the jumps tower over the riders as they first walk the course on foot to figure out striding and where they can make calculated turns to shave off seconds, Ashe makes no

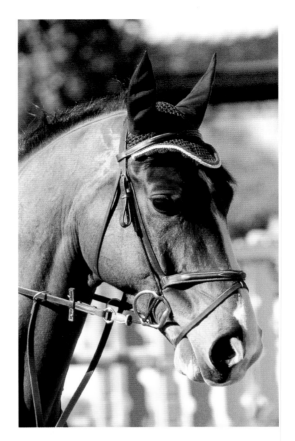

apologies for admitting she often asks herself if she's up to the task. "When I walk a Grand Prix course, I'm asking myself the ultimate question. After all these years of competing, riding, and jumping, I can feel it deep down in my soul, in the pit of my stomach: *Can I really do this?*" Perhaps that's what draws her to the sport—the personal challenge of one's own mettle. It's not whether you have the talent, it's whether you have the courage. "You either have this incredible desire and drive or you don't," says Ashe. "In jumpers, achieving that very personal accomplishment of communicating with my horse to become the best of the best at that moment in time is what appeals to me. You know, Arthur Ashe had his tennis racquet, Michael Jordan had his basketball, but in jumpers, it's me and my horse. We must be in sync. We must be a team."

Ashe revealed that her many years of experience hold her in good stead. Even though she always has a strategy for attacking every course, she says "you have to adjust your ride for everything that comes up on course. Experience allows you to salvage a game plan that goes awry." This is particularly true on the indoor circuit where the enclosed stadiums can convey an almost claustrophobic atmosphere. "The whole course almost seems kind of blurry. All the tests from the course designer come up so quickly, especially on an indoor course," says Ashe. Sometimes, the best friends a Grand Prix rider can have are natural ability and instinct.

IF VARIETY IS THE SPICE OF LIFE, IT IS ALSO

the main ingredient in the appeal of horse shows. For nearly every breed of horse or pony, there is an organization that maintains a registry of bloodlines and pedigreed breeding stock. With human nature being what it is, the owners of these blooded horses are compelled to occasionally gather and compete their horses. These breed shows are different from so-called open shows in one respect: open shows seek to award the best performance horse, regardless of the breed. Theoretically, an Arabian can compete against a quarter horse in a hunter class, but at breed shows, entries are limited to horses of a particular ilk—Arabians compete only against other Arabians, quarter horses against quarter horses. Plus, the breed shows seek to crown the best representatives of their registry; hence there's an added emphasis on how well a horse adheres to standards of conformation and movement.

Fortunately, the landscape of horse shows is painted with a palette of many different breeds. The benefit is that fanciers of equine breeds as disparate as Andalusians and hackneys, paso finos and Shetlands, and Morgans and Icelandic horses have events at which to indulge their passion. Every rider gets an opportunity to ride for a blue ribbon and to do it while mounted on a horse who in some way expresses a unique aspect of that rider's character and taste. Who can say what attracts one rider to a saddlebred, another to a Trakehner? Are they lured by the aesthetics of the breed or to the aura surrounding it? For whatever the reason, each breed of horse seems to draw its own aficionado.

It is said that horses with distinctive Appaloosa coloring have been depicted in prehistoric European cave paintings and in artwork dating back to imperialistic China. The Appaloosa's history with the Native American Nez Percé tribe is legendary. So it's not surprising that a heritage class, which celebrates the breed's significance in world history, is offered at Appaloosa shows. The heritage class is far more than a simple costume parade—participants take the event quite seriously, approaching it almost with a degree of reverence. Riders and their horses are attired in apparel and makeup that represents the contribution the Appaloosa made to historical events. Chinese emperors, Spanish conquistadors, even missionaries have been known to make appearances. Entrants perform as a group at the walk and trot, and then line up head to tail. As the judge individually examines each horse and rider, a brief but detailed description is read over the PA, evoking the theme and pertinence of the costume. To win, a competitor must be gifted in three areas: horsemanship, artistic vision, and historical accuracy—enthusiasm helps, too.

Marty Shaughnessy was first attracted to the heritage class when he and his wife attended the Appaloosa World Show in 1988. "I was drawn to the amount of work that went into the class—how much time and personal interest must have motivated the riders. And, I've always been kind of a history buff, so I found that part of the class appealing." Once enamored with the class, Shaughnessy quickly chose his costume—an Oglala Lakota war chief. "My generation was the one that grew up playing cowboys and Indians," says Shaughnessy. "I always thought that a Native American was a person to emulate, but I wanted to make sure I had all the authentic trappings in order to honor that image." It took three years for Shaughnessy and his wife to assemble the outfit for his heritage class. "Yeah, we made the traditional I-40 trading post tour," he revealed, alluding to the highway that

passes through the Southwest. "Let's just say we had a discerning eye. I'm very proud of my costume, especially a handmade black powder rifle." Shaughnessy has good reason to be proud. Besides winning ribbons in reining and western riding classes, he won the Men's Heritage Class at the 2000 Appaloosa World Show.

American saddlebreds have been called the peacocks of the show world, and it's not a misnomer. They do indeed appear to strut, inviting observers to look their way. They arch their necks and carry their tails aloft. There is no denying saddlebreds are fine examples of horseflesh, with their sinewy muscles that bulge beneath taut skin covered with hair no coarser than peach fuzz. The three-gaited variety is fine-boned—almost delicate—and flits like a sprite along the arena rail, hooves barely skimming earth. The five-gaited kin, blessed with a talent for the slow gait and the rack, is brawny and impressive with legs that rise and strike in a military cadence, firing like howitzers. As a breed, saddlebreds are aristocratic not pompous, flamboyant but not gaudy. Saddlebreds belong in the same luxury category as the diamond bracelet and the Oscar de la Renta evening gown.

Phoebe von Migula had a fascination with saddlebreds in her youth. As proof, she referred to her childhood scrapbook—the wish book of a horseless young girl. Pasted among the pages were photos of her dream horses—most of them displayed the trademark high-stepping action of a saddlebred. "I guess I was just drawn to them even then," says von Migula. As an adult, she lived in the same neighborhood as the Flintridge Riding Club, a famous hunter/jumper kingdom ruled by the venerable Jimmy Williams. It was inevitable that von Migula would be cajoled into buying a Thoroughbred hunter. "But once I got over being terrified of jumping, I realized I really didn't enjoy it. I still wanted

that darned saddlebred!" Eventually her dream became reality. She rode her horse Snow Summit to an AHSA (now USAEquestrian) Horse of the Year title in 1996. Then, while watching a weanling futurity, she spied a sweet-tempered pinto. "I remember saying to my trainer at the time, somewhat joking, 'There's my next western pleasure champion.' Little did I know that he'd be for sale as a four-year-old! When I saw his picture in an ad, I made the phone call and bought him." Destiny prevailed,

and von Migula and her horse Geronimo's Cadillac became blue ribbon winners. Von Migula scoffs at the misguided notion that saddlebreds are a temperamental breed. She works her own horse six days a week and is tutored by a trainer only at shows. By watching her compete her pinto, then feed the champ an armload of carrots, it's obvious there's only adoration in the eyes of both horse and human.

It's generally accepted that the Arabian is the world's oldest breed of domesticated horses. Originally prized by nomadic bedouin tribes, the Arabian is favored around the world for its undeniable charisma and extreme beauty. While many of its kind may resemble a porcelain doe-eyed creature, the Arabian is actually a hardy, spirited horse possessed with incredible stamina and a solid work ethic. It is also blessed with versatility. In the show ring, Arabians perform in events as varied as western pleasure, dressage, native costume displays, and ladies side saddle classes. Regardless of the particularities of the class, the Arabian is one of the rare breeds of show horses that is allowed—in fact, encouraged—to express itself. With its neck proudly arched and its tail held aloft, it's not difficult to imagine hot desert winds blowing through the Arabian's mane.

Laura Cronk was first introduced to Arabian show horses thirty years ago. "My mom rode Arabians when she was a girl, so it's fair to say I've been around them my whole life," says Cronk. "I've had the opportunity to train and show other breeds, but I was always drawn back to Arabians. They so enjoy human contact. We can show our Arabians all day, but the next morning they'll just about come inside and have a cup of coffee with you."

Cronk had the pleasure of handling and caring for the legendary Arabian stallion Khemosabi in his final years. Thoroughbred racehorses had Secretariat as their celebrity ambassador; Arabians had Khemosabi. He won national championships as the top Arabian stallion and as a western pleasure horse. It was an amazing feat, since one event is basically a halter class where the horse struts and poses for the judge on the end of a leadline, and the other is a performance class where the horse has to work graciously under tack. Rarely can an Arabian, especially a stallion, specialize in both. Beyond the blue ribbons, he went on to sire over 320 champions and currently reigns as

the most popular Arabian stallion of all time, having fathered nearly 1,300 offspring. These are staggering accomplishments for a homebred colt born literally in his owner's backyard. "When he was born, I wasn't thrilled," admitted Khemosabi's breeder, Ruth Husband. She was least impressed with the dark bay's extensive white markings. "I almost didn't bother to register him, but fortunately my husband is the horseman of the family, and he saw the colt's potential."

Throughout his show career, Khemosabi had a reputation for being calm and sedate in the warm-up ring but an exuberant performer in front of the crowds. Once the ingate swung open, he was like an actor walking onto a stage, ready to emote for his audience. When he first began his western pleasure career, Husband remembers being apprehensive. She recalls the young stallion being his cool self while warming up, but as the actual class approached, she was afraid he'd rear and walk around on his hind legs. "It turned out he was always the perfect gentleman.

He never misbehaved. It was as if he knew what he had to do to win," says Husband. The flashy bay seemed to thoroughly enjoy showing. While many horses become pensive on the road and go off their feed, Khemosabi usually gained weight, munching away on just about anything offered. "Yes, he was a walking mouth," laughs Husband. Khemosabi died just short of his thirty-fourth birthday, having spent years in semiretirement entertaining a steady stream of visitors from around the world. "When he was a tiny colt, he'd walk up behind me and shove his head under my arm," says Husband, explaining that the colt seemed to enjoy getting a hug from his human mom. That personable trait continued throughout his show ring career. "It's hard to explain, but if you looked into his eyes, he'd look right back at you. I truly believe there was a soul in there."

NOT EVERY HORSE SHOW AWARDING COLORED

ribbons to champion horses or medals to the top riders is of national importance. Some shows are significant only to the circle of horse lovers attending the event, whether they're members of a local riding club or boarders at the same stable. Names of these winners aren't posted on the Internet or plastered on the pages of self-congratulatory magazine ads. The judge might be the local itinerant riding instructor; the show grounds a dusty lot with pipe railing and a few trees. Experienced riders label these smaller offerings schooling shows because for them they serve no other purpose than a venue to educate a green horse. But to a significant percentage of competitors, these shows represent a worthy goal. A blue ribbon won here elicits the same response as if it represented a national championship. And well it should. For these are the riders, either neophytes or those struggling with a meager budget, who may become so impassioned with developing their competitive skills that they'll become tomorrow's venerated professionals and Olympic medalists.

It's a misconception that all of the elite, successful riders began their careers on high-dollar horses at posh country club settings. Many champions began in walk/trot classes on the backs of inexpensive, sturdy ponies or won their first blue ribbons at shows where the accompanying prizes were nothing more than bunches of carrots from local supermarkets. The horses at these shows may be nondescript, blessed with neither classy conformation nor elegance of movement, but they are, for the most part, trusty steeds happy to slog through the day's events. Upon their raw-boned backs sit riders clothed in hand-me-down riding habits, homemade jackets, and oversized boots. There's hardly a pair of custom chaps in sight. Yet their countenance is earnest: they are here to ride for a blue ribbon.

The day begins at dawn and continues until dusk. The ice chests and coolers, filled with rations to feed the troops, are stationed outside the open doors of horse trailers and pickup trucks, making it evident that it's going to be a marathon day.

By offering a daily high-point award, the show management tacitly encourages competitors to participate in a multitude of classes. And boy, are there plenty of classes! The show opens with simple halter classes where horses are led in by their handlers and judged on presentation and grooming. Euphemistically referred to as lead'em and feed'em events, these classes lend themselves to humorous interpretation. During the lineup, a Welsh pony seems to have amorous intentions toward his palomino neighbor and resists any tugging on his halter to pay attention. Yet a mere seven-year-old child can coerce a 1,000-pound quarter horse into posing like a plastic Breyer horse model.

Following the halter classes, it's a race back to the trailers where the horses are tacked up for their English events. Snaffles and kimberwickes come out of hiding as they're placed in the mouths of compliant horses—the arena soon to host a medley of colors. The Thoroughbreds and warmbloods, which populate the larger shows, are in short supply, replaced by more generic breeds and a dash of flash supplied by a pinto or an Appaloosa. As the horses are prompted into an animated trot, instructors and horse show moms line the rail and plead with their prodigies to check their diagonals, often to no avail. Whether it's an equitation class or one for hunters under saddle, the strategy doesn't change much. The English division culminates in a hunter hack class, which,

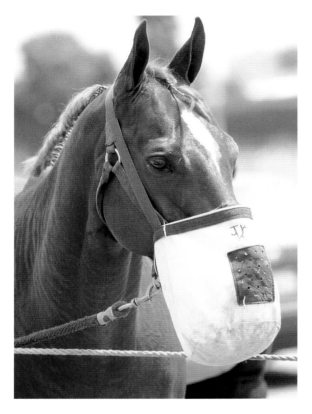

because of its deceptive simplicity, seduces nearly every exhibitor. A combination of flatwork and low jumping, it's a horse show axiom that the horses who perform beautifully at the walk, trot, and canter are the horses who balk at the jumps, vexing both judge and participants.

There's a short pause for a lunch break, which is when the ice chests and coolers are cracked open. Horses and ponies are tied either to the side of their trailers and pacified with well-stocked hay nets or tethered to picket lines with their muzzles buried in canvas feedbags. Either method keeps them content. Resigned to the routine, the horses and ponies cock their stifles and rest their legs knowing the end of siesta is near. In about thirty minutes, everyone's feeding frenzy is over. The resumption of the day's activities is heralded by the return of the newly invigorated judge climbing back into his crow's nest. In response, the march back to the show ring begins, only this time the horses are wearing western tack and the riders have switched into Wranglers and chaps. Few horse and rider pairs make the transition flawlessly. Generally there is some error in continuity that screams out Aha! An English hunter masquerading as a cowpony!

About the time the judge becomes bleary-eyed, the horse show parents frazzled, the riding instructors exasperated, and the horses ready to form a herd and bolt, the day ends with some sort of "fun" contest. This is a well-meaning effort to allow every exhibitor to go home with a ribbon; hence it has little to do with riding skill or the art of showmanship and everything to do with agility and determination. Whether it's a costume class or a gymkhana event, this last gasp of competition lures everyone still longing for a blue ribbon.

On this particular day, the final class is pole bending, a gymkhana game in which horse and rider must weave in and out of a series of poles anchored to the ground only by a coffee can filled with a large dollop of cement. With the stopwatch ticking away in the hand of a sun-baked volunteer, a young girl on an Appaloosa whomps her heels against her horse's sides and starts on course. Going away from the ingate, away from his four-legged friends, and away from the trailer (his shuttle home), the Appaloosa is lackluster, to say the least. His rider could probably run faster afoot. But once he turns the corner, his ears prick forward. Surely this must be his rider's final request for energy. So, with all the enthusiasm of a Thoroughbred in the homestretch, the speckled horse pins his ears and digs his striped hooves into the sandy footing at a gallop. As he weaves in and out of the poles, however, there's a slight misstep. Was he thinking too much of oats and a warm trailer ride rather than of stopwatches and precarious coffee cans? A pole bobbles, then falls to the ground. The weary onlookers, clinging to the arena fence for support after a long day, exhale a sigh of commiseration. It'd be nice if everyone could go home a winner. Yet such are the lessons of life.

Learning to show is synonymous with 4-H, which is geared for school-age riders under the age of eighteen. Despite being chided for their crisp white uniforms that evoke images of ice cream vendors or dairy technicians, 4-H competitors thrive in their organization's version of novice-level horse show competition. The volunteer-led agriculture program is not only best known for its nurturing of sheep and hog farmers but it also boasts a healthy corps of young equestrians. Following the traditions of 4-H, the members have to keep meticulous records of their horses' maintenance and any costs incurred. And it's a wonder those white uniforms stay so clean at horse shows: 4-H competitors are required to do all the grooming, schooling, and mucking themselves. "It became a habit to be organized," recalls Renee Kusler, now a medical student. "Plus, since I was responsible for all the care of my gelding, from brushing him to getting in the ring on time, I developed a really close bond with my horse. That paid off in the trail classes, because I felt like we really worked together," says Kusler. "My horse, Kaliente, became a willing partner in those events. Those obstacle courses required some really intricate movements. I had to tell him, 'Now put your foot right there. Now step over this.' It became a much more intimate relationship than I could have ever had with a human teammate in another sport. Besides, in 4-H horse shows your team leader or instructor isn't allowed to coach you from the rail. Talk about learning to ride!"

Chapter 8

GREEN AS GRASS

JUST AS NOVICE EQUESTRIANS HAVE TO START

out at small shows polishing their skills, horses have to learn their craft, too. While rated shows offer classes for green horses, it is not the venue where most make their debut. The nationally recognized horse shows are the Broadway of horse shows, and the schooling shows are the summer stock or repertory where young horses learn their roles. Only when the greenies can find their mark, walk onstage, and not be hypnotized by the audience can they headline at the major shows.

Not every rider has the fortitude to compete a green horse. It is a specialty best left to those who feel a calling to the vocation. The competitor who is showing a green horse must want the assignment because she relishes the personal challenge, not because she craves the spotlight. Though showmanship skills are important, what matters here isn't whether the rider can woo the judge but whether she can sweet-talk a coy young horse into doing his job. For just when the young horse offers a peek at his talent, he becomes obsessed with the mare standing next to him in the lineup or determines that the golf cart parked outside the back gate is the Chariot of Death. Such behavior often elicits the whining remark from a befuddled owner, "I don't understand his behavior. He's so good at home!"

When it comes to competing a green horse, riding for the blue is a distant goal. The blue ribbon is the buried treasure marked with an X on some mythical map—a trail of scratched classes littered along the path. Only those riders blessed with unending self-confidence and tireless patience should ever attempt the journey. "I know I can be on the best horse, quality and movement-wise at a show," says renowned quarter horse trainer Clay MacLeod, "but when they're green, they get so distracted by just about anything that they don't show themselves well, so they get beaten by a horse that just has more miles. That's the biggest challenge with the green ones, keeping them focused."

A rider on a green horse walks a tightrope. At the end, a sparkling blue ribbon beckons her. But on either side stretches a dark abyss. Within it lies that dreaded motion from the ring steward and the request, "Please excuse yourself because your horse is disrupting the rest of the class." Riders resort to concocting schedules to keep their greenies relaxed and focused. One tactic is to hand walk the horse repeatedly around the show grounds, allowing him to investigate the new surroundings. This can take hours because each time the greenie passes the judge's booth, he must stop and snort with amazement. To keep from wearing the actual rider down to exhaustion, a tag team is arranged. Each human contributing to the green horse's education chaperones one tour of the show grounds. Lead rope, complete with stud chain, is required.

Another choice is to court frostbite and get up before sunrise and longe the horse, letting him work off some high spirits before the competition begins. For the ultimate payoff, this venture should coincide with the advent of the show manager's offering of free donuts. They're meant for the ring crew, but one jelly donut can sustain the typical human through twenty minutes of predawn longeing.

Both these methods have to be handled with wisdom. Not enough longeing or hand walking and the youngster might come to life at the most inopportune time, such as when the judge is pinning the class. Yet, too much preparation and the horse isn't relaxed but browbeaten. Perhaps all riders of green horses should carry a note card tucked under their hats that bears the oft-quoted adage of a respected southern horsewoman. When she finds herself dealing with a green show horse who just won't settle down to business, she keeps her sanity by accepting that "sometimes you just gotta dance with the boy you came with."

By all accounts I am a rare breed of individual on the show circuit. Although I am an amateur rider, I train and compete my own homebred horses. That means I have to put up with all the nonsense that goes along with showing green horses. While my chosen discipline is hunt-seat, the experiences I've had on my colts and fillies share universal themes with anyone else undertaking the

schooling of a young show horse regardless the style of saddle they ride in. No doubt some sort of emotional support group would be popular. It could be called GRASS: Greenie Riders' Assistance and Support System. There'd be monthly meetings to unleash woebegone tales. When a member stands up and explains with halting speech how her normally placid four-year-old arrived at the show grounds, stepped off the trailer, and immediately morphed into a fire-breathing dragon, everyone could all join hands, shake their heads knowingly and sigh sympathetically, "We understand."

Sometimes the only reward I get for a day of showing is an appreciative comment from a familiar equestrian at the back gate. "You never seem to get upset" is something I often hear. What else am I to do in response to the occasional pitching fit on course or the sudden spook in the corner? Such antics just go with the territory. Yet though I acknowledge the futility of it all, something deep in the core of my existence propels me back into that show ring once again. It's the lure of that ten-inch slice of royal blue satin, as ethereal as it seems. Like a specter mentoring me from another world, I can hear a voice coaxing me down the final line of jumps (a wall to an oxer), *If you can just finesse it, just loop the reins just a tad, you might be in the hunt for the blue.* It's at that moment that my greenie lands after the oxer, dives into my hands against his snaffle, does a loop-de-loop, and nearly tosses me out of the tack. I can just hear my friends sighing from the grandstand, *Darn. She was doing so well.*

When I trudge past another amateur, wisely mounted on a certified packer, she remarks, "Well, at least when you do win something, you know you earned it." It takes me the entire trek back to the shedrow to decipher the hidden meaning of that faint praise. While I unsaddle my horse, who seems quite pleased with himself, I contemplate giving up. But then, forever the optimist (a requirement if one is to ride green horses), I hear that little voice again, encouraging me to take a breather, wipe down my boots, and tack up again. *The under saddle class,* the voice whispers, *maybe you can win the hack.*

Chapter 9

BEHIND THE SCENES

NO RIDER BECOMES A BLUE RIBBON WINNER

just by wishing and daydreaming; no fairy godmother is going to wave her magic wand and—poof—make her a champion. To become a winner in the show ring, a competitor must have the look of a winner. And it's far more than just a set of fancy clothes and a thousand-dollar saddle. If a rider seriously hopes to ride for the blue, she must dedicate herself to long hours of preparation.

Most riders use a dress rehearsal to prepare for competition. A riding instructor or trainer orchestrates the dress rehearsal. It doesn't matter whether the discipline is western or English, dressage or saddleseat, the trainer or instructor's job is to coach his or her students into knowing their roles by heart: you enter the arena in this manner, you hit your mark at such-and-such a point, deliver a captivating performance, and exit gracefully. Like ballet dancers, riders are repeatedly contorted into their classic, basic positions until muscle memory takes over and the English rider's heels are instinctively pressed down; the western rider's back becomes ramrod straight. Proper form must become instinctual so that the rider's mind is free to improvise in the show ring, whether to add a flourish that will impress the judge or to salvage a misstep.

As a weekend competition approaches, riding lessons take on a much more serious tone. Depending on the trainer's temperament and the rider's ego, the motivational tactics include coercion, pleading, blackmail, histrionics, and personal assaults on the student's character. "Your horse isn't listening to you in the line, Elizabeth," comes the admonishment from the trainer. "Your second fence is too rushed. Jump in once more, ask your horse to wait on stride three, and if he doesn't, pull him up!" Elizabeth is not successful. She won't win many blues—or ribbons of any color—if her horse continues to tune out her requests. "Elizabeth! Now trot into your first fence and *make him* listen to you by adding a stride." The frustration is evident as the demands take on a more plaintive appeal. "Elizabeth, we aren't quitting until you get this right. I have a dental appointment on Wednesday. Shall I call and cancel it?"

While riders must learn how to present themselves as skilled thespians, the horses must be kept sharp as well. This demands that the trainer regularly ride the horse to critique the mount's weak spots. There's no point in rehearsing the entire script—that drains the performance of any creative spark. Instead, the trainer of a show jumper directs the horse to demonstrate a little more panache over the jumps by schooling him through a grid (a tricky set of jumps that elicits a horse's gymnastic skills). Or perhaps a quarter horse used for horsemanship classes is a tad sticky on his flying changes. The western trainer reenacts the horse's last performance, analyzes just where the miscommunication occurred, and explains the nuances of flying leads to the horse: Once again, please, but with more feeling.

It would be difficult to recognize the stars of the equestrian world in these daily rehearsals. Just like actors caught out in public, free of makeup and wardrobe, you could be standing next to a champion and not even realize it. Underneath a fuzzy saddle pad draped in split-leather tack is the western pleasure champ from last year's World Show. Who'd have recognized the gelding with his tail braided and knotted to keep it free from sand and tangles? Could that be last month's medal winner sitting atop her horse, a frayed ponytail spilling down her back? Is that a hunt-seat competitor or a western rider? It's hard to tell, especially with the schizophrenic fashion choice of pairing leather schooling chaps with a velvet hunt cap. There is no glamour outside the rays of the spotlight. It's saved for show time.

For many riders, particularly those of timid nature or those mounted on sensitive animals, the warm-up ring is the scariest place on the show grounds. Like warring factions from different homelands, riders engage in a battle for one last attempt at the practice jump or negotiate for territorial rights to make a final sweeping pass down the long side of the rail. Time is running out for last-minute preparations, and everyone wants to end their schooling on a perfect note to boost their confidence. It's often said that there's no greater guarantee of disaster in the show ring than a disastrous warm-up, and the knowledge of that axiom can be seen in a rider's face. So the tactics become cutthroat. She who hesitates in the warm-up ring is not only lost but also frequently body-slammed by a more aggressive competitor. Adding to the chaos are the kids on ponies who zip in and out from between the legs of the much larger equines. And then there are the Oblivious Ones, riders who seem zoned out, so totally focused on flatwork that they do not recognize their concentric circles intersect with nearly everyone else's path of trajectory. Perhaps this all is as it should be. Ultimately, the turmoil of the warm-up ring serves to make the environment of the show arena a comparative haven of tranquility.

Equestrians often contemplate the paradox that so much expense and attention is given to the main show arena, yet the actual place for preparation—the warm-up ring—often resembles a battlefield. Furthermore, if they're searching for a place to longe a fresh horse (so that they don't add to the melee), they'll likely have to first find the designated longeing area. Oh yes, that would be a fifteen-minute hike due east to the back corner of the parking lot, on the gravel, next to the freeway.

Besides the dress rehearsal, a rider must also prepare for the aesthetics of the competition. The winning look would not be complete without grooming the horse to a sheen equal to that of a burnished brass lantern. After all, this is not an impromptu performance: Competitors have chosen to strut their horses before the scrutinizing eyes of a judge. All can sense the pride of ownership. "Here, look at my lovely animal," says the rider. "I've been planning for this occasion for weeks."

There is no shortage of products on the market to aid in the beautification process. Got a frazzled mane? No problem. Spritz on some detangler, comb through, and your horse now sports a mane Rapunzel would envy. Have a gray horse with a fondness for rolling in soiled bedding the night before your class? Does he seem to guffaw at your attempts to keep him silvery white? There are several choices here, ranging from midday sessions at the shampoo bowl to secret formulas that fizz away those nasty green and yellow spots. From flannel rub rags that knock off the final specks of dust to aloe-based gels that add glistening highlights to a soft muzzle, the grooming equipment that accompanies every show horse rivals the makeup collection of a Hollywood starlet.

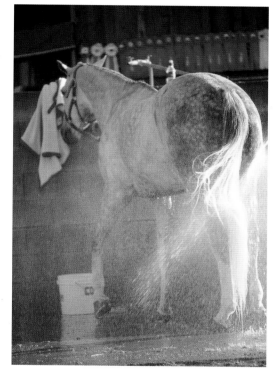

The unsung heroes at the back gate—or back at the trailer or barn—are the grooms themselves. They are the tireless ones who glorify horse and rider, while they themselves look as if they're ready for either rehab or resuscitation. The horses may be spot free, but the grooms have hoof oil splattered on their jeans, blue gooey shampoo under their fingernails, and a plastic mane comb jammed into their back pocket. It's not a glamorous job. Most full-time grooms are working students, serving as interns to a top trainer, or Hispanic immigrants earning an honest living doing a job most native-born workers would shun after one shift. Yet both interns and immigrants have an affinity for working with horses and often develop a close relationship with the equines in their care. Who knows a horse better than the person who combs out the animal's tail strand-by-strand, sponges off the sweat of saddle marks, and stands for hours in the role of human hitching post?

Chapter 10

A Trainer's Life

IT'S 7:00 A.M. AND SUSAN SMITH HAS BEEN

awake and on her feet for two hours. The dew still clings to the wheel wells of her horse trailer, although she knows that within a short time the sun will evaporate both the moisture and all hopes for a cool day. She checks the pocket of her jacket. Yup, her sunglasses are handy. So is her tube of lip balm. She begins to calculate the distance from the parking lot to the entry booth, but then, with a shrug, resigns herself to the fact that it doesn't much matter. She'll trudge the pathway countless times until the toes of her paddock boots know the route through the grass and brambles by heart.

Right now her main concern is whether or not her students will get their mounts ready in time for their first classes. It's late summer, and this is the final opportunity to qualify for the year-end championship show. It's do-or-die time for one of her young charges. The eleven-year-old girl is aboard her new horse and is still struggling to get acquainted with her horse's long stride and nonchalant attitude toward the jumps. If she doesn't pin in her hunter classes today, she won't be accompanying the barn to the season finale.

"Kristen!" calls Smith from atop the knoll. "Honey, you've got to get Oliver tacked up or you're going to miss your class." The young girl stops longeing her bay gelding, reels in the cotton rope, and heads back up to the trailer. Smith doesn't offer grooming services to her students. She believes part of horsemanship is learning to care for your own animal. It can put a crimp in leisure time at shows, but there's little time to dally in the warm-up ring when blue ribbons are on the line.

As the day progresses, Smith shirks off her jacket, dons her sunglasses, and continually gulps from a bottle of ice water. The fare at the concession stand has switched from egg burritos to grilled burgers, but Susan will be lucky to grab a soda and a bag of chips. She's forever mobile, but it's hard to lose her at a show. She can always be found at one of three places: the warm-up ring, the trailer, or her current spot—alongside the rail. Blatant coaching from the sidelines is frowned upon, but that doesn't prevent Smith from vicariously riding each round with each of her students. She counts the strides between jumps under her breath and telepathically cues her client's horse for a lead change with a perceptible nudge of her leg. When one of her adult amateur riders, an experienced horsewoman aboard a young horse, struggles through a round of green hunters, Smith knows to offer the barest of criticism: The woman already knows what went well and what to fix. With this type of rider, Smith's job is to function more as a mentor or an empathetic friend than as a trainer. But when young Kristen misjudges the takeoff to a jump and causes her horse to chip into a line, Smith slaps the palm of her hand against the arena rail. The youngster will get an earful when she exits the ring. The girl is full of promise but is still learning that one split-second lapse of judgment can cost her a ribbon in a tough class. "Sometimes," laments Smith, "I feel like I can't make them want it bad enough."

Most professional trainers begin as horse crazy teenagers who, upon graduating from high school and the junior ranks of show ring competition, make the choice to pursue a career on horseback. Surprisingly, a good percentage first earn college degrees. The diplomas sit gathering dust, serving only as insurance policies should the horse training gig turn sour.

A few horse trainers reach the rarified stratosphere of national recognition where show barns run as well-oiled machinery, replete with assistants, stable managers, and professional grooms. Such trainers of the royal realm are perpetually within arm's reach of their cell phones and their golf carts: one connects them to their bloodstock agent or stockbroker, the other to their clients at the back gate. But the vast majority of trainers hover at the middle-income range. They are the blue-collar work-

ers—the backbone of the industry—toiling to keep the horse shows supplied with an annual crop of green riders. Often they make financial ends meet only because a spouse is earning a reliable income in the real world. Others teeter on the brink—a tumble from a rank horse can end their careers with few resources to cushion the fall. One must feel a calling to the profession, perhaps as one does toward other vocations that reward the devotee with little more than personal satisfaction.

"My life is hectic," says Steve Cruse, a soft-spoken Appaloosa and quarter horse trainer. "From July to mid-September, I'm on the road showing ten out of twelve weeks. Plus, the show season overlaps with breeding season on the ranch. We can breed up to 165 mares a year." But hectic schedules aren't his only concern. Managing a barn of highly motivated clients remains his biggest challenge. "That's the toughest part of my job," admits Cruse. "There's a lot of competition within my own barn. The kids are great, but sometimes it's the parents in the background, driving the kids, that get to be a problem. This is an expensive sport. I understand why my customers want to win. But sometimes it can get too competitive, especially with twenty-five different owners in the barn. Showing is supposed to be fun, you know."

Cruse further explained that two competitions are often being waged: the battle in the show ring for blue ribbons and the battle behind the scenes, within his own barn, between various owners for supremacy. Fortunately, with his inimitable, laid-back style, Cruse is able to ride herd on his clients and keep everyone happy without playing favorites. Such a feat only points out the need for people skills if a trainer is to succeed. For example, to retain customers, trainers must know when to stroke the ego of a struggling rider and when to jump-start his or her competitive spirit with a tongue lashing. They have to be poised to deliver an impromptu locker-room pep talk whenever the team looks ready to slink back to the trailer in defeat. And, they must be blessed with thick skin, for nowhere in the horse show world is there any guarantee of loyalty. The penniless kid who was plucked from the pony classes and nurtured as a protégé will walk away when Olympic dreams seem more attainable one shedrow over. Sometimes all a trainer can do is find solace in knowing that he was the one who led the rider to her first blue ribbon.

On the other hand, ask a group of show riders to divvy up dirt about their trainers, and you're liable to get an earful. Naturally, none of the riders wanted to speak on the record, lest she find her tack trunk cast into the barn aisle and her horse left tied to the nearest sycamore. But during a roundtable discussion in which people were assured of being anonymous, it became evident that riders have quite a lot of pent-up hostilities—and humor—to vent. The most prominent recurring theme was control. Most show horse trainers are, as one rider described, "rabid control freaks." According to the group of riders, trainers want their horses turned-out a certain way, as if they belong to some elite cavalry regiment. And, the trainer's barn, regardless of location, is managed with the iron fist of a feudal king. One girl told how her trainer demanded that the radio be kept tuned to only country music stations. It didn't matter whether the grooms were braiding horses at midnight or if the trainer was even on the premises, it was country music or nothing. Another rider topped that by announcing that her trainer controlled not only the station but also the volume on the radio by securing the knobs with layers of silver duct tape.

Is it a conspiracy? Are successful trainers control-crazy because they jealously guard their proven recipe for blue ribbons, afraid to stray from the menu? Or do they run their barns like drill sergeants, fearful that too much creative thinking on their clients' part might lead to anarchy? "Once I overheard my trainer talking to another trainer in the warm-up ring at an A show," confesses an amateur jumper rider. "I'm not sure exactly what they were discussing, but I distinctly heard my trainer say, and he wasn't kidding, 'This is the only business where the customer is always wrong.'"

Dressage riders seem to take the brunt of their trainer's obsession with control—as it should be since the discipline of dressage is born of precision and compliance. One young rider related how her dressage instructor rebuked her for using an indirect rein. "She threatened me and said if I did it one more time she'd throw a rock at me. I thought she was kidding, but sure enough, the next time I made a bad attempt at a leg yield, a piece of granite ricocheted off my leg."

Chapter 11

THE JUNIOR YEARS

IN HORSE SHOW TERMINOLOGY, RIDERS YOUNGER

than eighteen (or nineteen in some riding associations) are classified as juniors. This group of riders is allowed its own age division designed to create a fair playing field. There's a touch of irony to this. More than a few juniors could no doubt outride the older professionals who have become lax in their skills. And the nonchalant amateur adults have little desire to muster the amount of zeal the young riders possess. In other words, don't let the blond pigtails, the pink hair ribbons, or the young fellow who resembles a diminutive CEO fool you. These kids are tough, savvy competitors.

Hard lessons are learned from the first forays into the show ring. Even if a junior rider is merely ambling through a walk/jog class on the back of an ancient pony, she'll be determined to capture the eyes of the judge if she wants to win a ribbon. So, she develops the maneuvering skills of a Le Mans driver. She's taught that first impressions do count, so her entrance into the show arena takes on all the fanfare of a Las Vegas act. A sweet smile may endear her to the horse show secretary, but it doesn't win her ribbons. Hence, junior riders develop a game face, a stoic grimace that makes them nearly unrecognizable even to their own parents.

By the time they reach adolescence, junior riders become either poised equestrians in the show ring or they fade from the scene. They can be lured away by the demands of school, a lack of finances, or the siren's song of young love. Those who choose to stay have to deal with their teenage angst inside the horse world. Such challenges only compound the pressures of competing on a show circuit. If a rider is fortunate, she will have a mentor or a trainer who keeps her focused on her horsemanship.

"Between the ages of twelve and fourteen the girls can be difficult," explains hunter/jumper trainer Karole Caldwell, who always seems to have a barn full of young girls and teenagers. "As a riding instructor and horse trainer, I face the same tribulations as the parents and the schoolteachers: the talking back to authority figures, the teary outbursts, and the little attempts at rebellion. I have to take them [the students] aside and explain that I simply will not tolerate that kind of behavior. I nip it in the bud. For example, if the boyfriend starts to show up at the barn, that's fine. But if he shows up, and then the girl comes for her lesson wearing a halter top with her boots and breeches, well, I've got to draw the line. We're here to ride, not to entertain our beaus," says Caldwell. "And then sometimes, I feel like a camp counselor. Their self-esteem is so fragile. Their egos can rise and fall, depending on how well they did at a show."

Besides the social stresses, junior riders often have to juggle schoolwork and family responsibilities with their love for horses and aspirations for show ring competition. True, there are some prominent juniors who seem to have all the perks. Born of wealthy parents, they have tutors accompanying them to shows and grooms preparing their horses, but they are certainly not the norm. Far more teens have to struggle to maintain a link to their passion.

Rebecca Prince is fifteen and competes her Thoroughbred, Remember Paris, in junior hunter/jumper classes. Taught by her trainer to be self-reliant, she does all the dirty work herself at shows, from grooming Paris to mucking his stall. She claims she doesn't mind the extra work. It makes her feel closer to her horse and improves her horsekeeping skills. Lithe and fresh-faced, she's still shy around boys and unencumbered by romantic entanglements. But, she has to be creative to stay on the show circuit. "Any extra money I get, I put it toward show expenses like equipment that I might need. It took me a while to save up, but recently I bought Paris a new bridle. I'm too young to work much, but a family friend owns a Chinese restaurant so they let me occasionally bus tables. Not very

glamorous," she admits, "but it's a way to earn money. That's probably my biggest worry: how can I afford to show? My parents really help me out, so if I don't do well, I start to feel guilty. I start to think I'm wasting my parents' money. My dad loves me so much that even in hard times he'll put out the money so I can show. He said he really enjoys seeing my riding career blossoming. So, if I think I've done poorly at a show because I missed a lesson, or I didn't prepare enough in the schooling ring, I get really down on myself. That's the worst feeling of all." It's amazing that with such internalized pressures Rebecca has the emotional fortitude to be a winning rider.

Such single-minded focus is not rare among juniors. Nineteen-year-old Allison Carroll, a champion paint horse competitor, always knew what she wanted. In her final year as a junior, she wanted to go out on top by winning classes at the Paint World Show in Fort Worth, Texas. "I don't think I've ever wanted anything so badly," says Allison. "For months ahead of time, all I could think about was riding in those classes. I could just see myself riding the pattern—for western riding— and winning that blue ribbon and that belt buckle." No doubt, she'd paid her dues. "In this sport, you slowly inch your way up to the top. It takes years to get into the swing of things, to know exactly what it takes to win, to develop those winning skills. I'd shown paints for years. During show season, I'd leave school in midweek to compete in a show that ran through the weekend," reveals Allison. "Needless to say, I missed a lot of school that I had to make up."

Paired with her horse, Shine My Zipper, whom she describes as "a horse with a ton of personality and an incredible sweet tooth for all kinds of hard candy," Allison became a force to be reckoned with. She won both the 14-18 western pleasure and western riding classes at the 2000 World Show, and she was announced the high point western youth rider. "Now that—the high point award—was a

total surprise because I didn't know I'd passed up my closest rival in the point standings. Was I happy? Let's just say I sat down and cried nonstop for, oh, about half an hour. It was what I'd dreamed of for so long. And it all came true."

Sacrifices and unwavering dedication are admirable, but they sometimes take their toll. Unless they've made the choice—and have had the opportunity—to step into a professional riding career, riders who've graduated from the junior ranks often feel adrift. College may await them, but with that comes the heartbreaking decision of what to do with the horse who carried them to so many victories. Sell or lease him to another younger junior? Or pension him out in semiretirement, which may be a waste of a sound, trained show horse? Some nineteen- and twenty-year-olds express a sense of playing catch-up with their nonequestrian peers who are already firmly rooted in college majors and business internships. Then there's the challenge of resurrecting a social life. Attracting the opposite sex is a daunting task when your best duds are your one pair of jeans unsoiled by tack soap or boot polish. Yet most who've survived the transition from the junior years of showing into the "real world" have no regrets. The years spent pursuing blue ribbons taught them life lessons that can't be found in textbooks: love your horse, treat him with respect, and he'll never let you down. Exude self-confidence, yet give respect where it's due, and you'll come out a winner every time.

Chapter 12

Dogs, Kids, and Ponies

THERE'S AN OLD SAYING IN RURAL HORSE

country that "Dogs, kids, and ponies will make a liar out of you every time." In other words, just when you're wrangling for bragging rights, your obedient dog will refuse to sit up and bark, your angelic child will burst into a demonic tantrum, and your bombproof pony will suddenly become a raging beast. Despite their propensity for calamity, all three are an integral part of the horse show landscape. It'd be a much more boring affair without dogs, kids, and ponies.

Like most lifelong horse show competitors, I have many a tale to tell about horse show dogs. I had Tony, the rescued greyhound who could never quite detox from his race training. At a national horse show where one arena was set on an open turf field, he broke away from me when he spied an errant jackrabbit. The entire show was held up until I could no longer ignore the pleas from the announcer, "Will the owner of that greyhound please contain him? He's coursing a rabbit on the derby field, and we can't start the medal class." All eyes turned to me as I slunk toward the distant blur of hound and hare.

Then there was Sugar, a fluffy white fur ball of a Samoyed. He had a bit of a finicky appetite for a horse show dog, meaning he wasn't keen on tacos at lunchtime, but he made a marvelous foot warmer. During evening classes, when we perched in the grandstands to watch our buddies ride, we coaxed him into lying across our feet. He was like a pair of giant fuzzy bedroom slippers.

And, I can't forget Nancy, the Old English sheepdog—a most unusual breed for a horse show dog. Like a dust mop she collected bits of hay, dirt, and shavings, but she was a fierce protector. My sister and I could sleep on cots in the tack room at night, and Nancy would stand guard, defying anyone to enter unannounced.

But the most memorable are Kiwi and Maori, my sister's two Jack Russell terriers. They are swaggering examples of why the breed is not for everyone. On the one hand, they are perpetually amusing. They can devise a game by snapping at buzzing flies or hunt for hours for the phantom varmint that lurks in the haystack. But they are also determined to be the center of attention. More than once (like others of their brethren) they have disrupted a hack class because they've darted through the fence as horses trotted past.

Because of their unpredictable behavior, horse show managers are beginning to crack down on unruly dogs. Some shows cite a $100 impound fee for any dog caught off a leash. A dog can be a problem—especially if he incites a horse to spook—as well as a nuisance.

It's hard to reform a dog once he's learned to mooch from the horse show concession stand. At a recent show, a portly yellow lab with a continual string of anticipatory drool dangling from his lips apparently was unaware that he wore a sign around his collar that read, "I am too fat. Please do not feed me." Yet horse show dogs will never vanish from the scene. Why? Because the horse show dog is nearly as indispensable as the tack trunk, the tote box of brushes, and the zippered garment bag. The dog, you see, is also an accessory. The only difference is that, unlike the collection of color-coded,

monogrammed inanimate objects, the dog is a wellspring of affection and comfort to anyone with a pair of boots who looks like she has had a rough day in the saddle. Haven't won a blue ribbon all weekend? The resident barn dog will lick your wounds. Need to vent some cynicism toward the course designer, the judge, or the cranky guy at the back gate? Canine ears are the most attentive. And just when you think there is no joy to be found in your Shakespearian tragedy of a competition, your dog will happily provide some comic relief.

And then there are little kids and ponies, who seem forever engaged in a battle of wills. Rarely is either one the victor for long. Though it may seem that the child has the upper hand and is able to maneuver the pony from one end of the show arena to the other, the pony is merely biding his time,

awaiting that golden moment of opportunity when he can seize the bit in his teeth and forge his own path to that oasis of leisure time—the center of the arena. *I believe we shall eventually line up here*, the pony seems to be saying beneath his bushy forelock, *so I'll just hang out and wait for the rest of you.* No matter how much the child pulls and twists on the rein or thumps on the pony's side with the heel of a tiny boot, the pony remains steadfast. The cries of "Cluck to him!" or "Make him go forward!" chorused from the sidelines do little more than delight the obstinate pony and embarrass the grimacing child.

After all, what can an adult really do to a pony? They're too large to climb aboard and school. Often, the only choice is to strike some sort of compromise: the pony agrees to pack the child around the show ring at a safe and reasonable speed for no more than three minutes at a time in return for a large portion of carrots, hugs, and alfalfa, and is treated like the little prince that he is. Occasionally, the pony will renege on his end of the bargain. In this case, the services of an equestrian gunslinger are called upon. An older junior rider, a graduate of the pony ranks herself and wise to the orneriness of pesky ponies, arrives on the scene. She evokes the spirit of Wyatt Earp, strutting with spurs jangling into a dusty ranch town that's in need of vigilante justice. As she climbs aboard, her crop drawn like a six-shooter, the look in the pony's eyes changes from aloofness to dread. Listen closely and you can almost hear a pony-sized voice utter, *uh-oh.* Rarely does the altercation result in a quick draw contest in the center of town. Usually the pony complies quickly, disarming himself and being the good little pony he was originally trained to be. After all, ponies are pretty smart, otherwise their ancestors wouldn't have been wily enough to survive the harsh conditions of their native homelands. So, once the rules for behavior are reestablished, the pony relents and returns to being the pawn of his child rider—at least for a while.

Barbara Sackett, a former show rider, recalls a story about her own duel with a noncompliant pony and a frustrated child. A local pony club was having its annual event, and it offered an entire division of children's walk/trot classes. It seemed like a good introduction to competition for her daughter, Monica, especially since Sackett had been looking forward to exploring the role of horse show mom. So the day was planned. Monica was mounted on the family's pinto pony mare, a Shetland cross whose position on the hierarchy of domestic duties ranked between pet and lawn ornament. The pony, Patches, was a tad overfed and underworked. But, she was trustworthy enough to be ridden along the neighborhood streets, so surely she'd pack young Monica around her first course of tiny cross-country obstacles. Well, perhaps. Sackett stood just outside the barriers of the course, and watched as daughter and pony traipsed down the marked trail and over little sunken logs and a few natural hedges. Just as she was envisioning a possible blue ribbon for the pair, the two disappeared into a covey of trees. Sackett waited, but neither pony nor child emerged for the next obstacle. Suddenly, there was the unmistakable cry of a child for her mother, and Sackett waded through knee-high brambles to find Monica plopped on the ground beside Patches. The girl was unhurt but infuriated with the potbellied pinto. The mare had absolutely refused to step over a small pile of logs, and when urged, had whirled and unseated her rider. Now Patches stood motionless, ears defiant, muzzle pursed, and legs locked in place. Like the cottonwood trees around her, Patches was planted. Being a woman of action, Sackett ordered her daughter back in the saddle, "I told her to stop crying and that she was going to get around the course one way or another." To prove her determination, Sackett grabbed the reins and began leading the grumpy pony and teary-eyed child over the logs. It must've been quite a sight—a mother out on the course leading pony and child despite protestations from both. They did finish the entire event in a leadline sort of manner. Even ponies should know that Mom always wins.

Chapter 13

Horse Show Moms

THEY CAN TAKE APART A PONY'S BRIDLE AND

switch it from snaffle to Pelham in less than five minutes. They've memorized the fine print of an entry form and can usually chisel a few dollars off a show bill during a tête-à-tête with the office secretary. They have enough fashion sense to dress up an exhibitor like a runway model, yet enough chutzpah to dress down an unwary judge who crosses their path. Give them a rub rag, and they'll shine your boots. Give them a day's notice, and they'll whip up enough home-cooked food to feed an army, pack it into an ice chest, and even bring along a tablecloth and plastic forks. Step aside ye of demure demeanor. It's show time, and the brigade of horse show moms is on the grounds.

Few would argue the adage that behind every dedicated show rider is a dedicated horse show mom. The typical horse show mom is forever caught up in the moment, oblivious to the fact that her Ralph Lauren blouse is stained with horse goobers and her hair sports a halo of alfalfa. If her child, regardless of age, is about to enter the show ring with a dusty horse, it's Super Horse Show Mom to the rescue. She's not adverse to elbowing her way through a crowd of 16-hand horses or running a dandy brush over a horse's haunches. In a pinch, she can even oil a quartet of hooves.

Though most horse show moms have never piloted a horse much beyond a plodding walk, over the seasons they've acquired enough expertise to sit in grand-stands and pin classes with about the same accuracy as the judges. They not only know the jargon but they also understand it and make no apologies for voicing their descriptive opinions. More than one horse show mom has listened to the ribbons being announced and guffawed at the results. It's not uncommon to overhear mom-isms such as "How could that bay gelding place above my kid? It two-tracked down the rail and was above the bit the whole second direction!"

Unsuspecting judges may bear the brunt of a horse show mom's anger whenever the class results don't reflect her instincts. See that fellow cowering behind the shadow of the ring steward? Yes, that would be the judge slinking away on a break following the pony class. Is a mother's interpretation of the class results clouded by maternal love? Perhaps, but it's hard to argue with the opinions of any woman who's spent years serving her offspring as coach, groom, private caterer, motivational speaker, personal secretary, and mental health counselor. "Why can't the judges all go to the same school of judging?" asks Marcia Calderon, horse show mom to her daughter, Krista, who has been on the Appaloosa circuit for nearly a decade. "Sometimes, when I see that there are just questionable decisions being made, well, my blood just boils inside. But we're trying to teach our kids sportsmanship, right? I mean, I don't want to just lose it and become this crazed Little League mom."

A horse show mom trying to keep her comments to herself is a trait lacking in many horse show moms. More than once an exuberant mom has overstepped the boundary of benevolent cheerleader by erupting with a resounding exclamation of joy when her child's rival goes off course in a championship class. No one chastises the horse show mom for such an outburst: it's understandable given the emotional and financial investments she's made. Just as pointed are the often unwanted tidbits of motherly advice. No one is immune. Teenagers are harangued about keeping their shoulders back in an equitation class. Short stirrup kids must learn to ignore their moms coaching them from the rail, especially when such instructions contradict those of their trainer. My own horse show mom is no exception. Once she came to watch me compete a new horse I was showing for my trainer. The horse was quite keen and required a steady, focused ride. As I cantered down to a large oxer, my legs and

hands rating the hot tamale gelding to a perfect spot, I heard my mom along the rail utter in a concerned, yet authoritative, tone, "You know, Cindy, that jump is pretty high." Oh, there's nothing like losing your focus at the moment of take off.

Beyond providing unsolicited show ring commentary and performing the domestic chores of securing food for horse and child, the horse show mom is afforded one other official duty, that of horse show historian. Despite her best maternal efforts, this most important mission often ends with Mom becoming a figure of comic relief. The duty of historian involves recording the triumphs of the day's competition. The tools required are either an automatic-focus camera (for candid still shots) or a video camera (to immortalize an entire class routine). Yet both, when in the hands of a horse show mom, are fraught with the potential for disaster. Despite the guarantee that the 35mm camera is of the "point and shoot" variety, chances are the snapshots will reveal a mother's thumb over the lens or an off-kilter montage of disembodied heads and floating horse ears—the only vestiges of a glorious blue ribbon–winning moment. Place a video camera in a mother's hands and you're likely to unleash a budding auteur. What was supposed to be a mere recording of a single class turns into a fifty-minute documentary of epic proportions. The tape opens with a panoramic vista of the show grounds and a zoom shot of every identifiable spectator. Then, the scene is set while the camera records the activity at the back gate as her film's star, her child, is readied for the class. Of course, this vision is accompanied by the horse show mom's continual narration, which is replete with commentary about the weather, the dinner they ate last night, and an appraisal of the bathroom facilities. Then, just as the program is about to reach its climax, and the star is about to make her entrance, the battery goes dead.

If the show ring is a microcosm for life where participants are faced with physical stress, emotional upheavals, and tests of character, who better to hold your hand along the way than your mom? And when you're successful, who better to congratulate you than the person who schlepped your tack and riding clothes from horse trailer to the back gate a million times?

International Grand Prix jumper rider Molly Ashe has a unique perspective on horse show moms. Her mother, Sue, is a noted judge and professional horsewoman, but she was also Molly's trainer throughout most of her junior years. "My mom was the driving force in my junior years. She was never going to accept anything less than the best from me, so there were times when the relationship was a bit rocky," admits Ashe. "But because of my mom, I learned that horse shows can teach you a lot about life. First, life is not always fair. No matter how much you plan, how much you dream, things can still go wrong. Second, I learned to accept defeat. You aren't always going to get what you want. Probably at the time, I didn't appreciate all that my mom did for me, but now not a day goes by that I don't realize it, and I thank her every chance I get."

Ashe describes one incident with her horse show mom as being "like something out of a storybook." Though Ashe was already a successful rider on the Grand Prix circuit, Sue's schedule never coincided with her daughter's performances until the Devon, Pennsylvania, horse show in 2001. Ashe had gone clean in the Grand Prix's first round and was preparing for the jump-off. "My mom was judging hunters in the other ring, so I knew she was there, somewhere. I went last in the jump-off, so there was all this suspense. Then, when I knew I'd won, I was swamped as I came out of the gate. Everyone was congratulating me. I was being asked by ESPN to give an interview, but I was more concerned because I couldn't find my mom in the crowd. That was the most important thing to me. I was getting kind of choked up, thinking, 'Where is she? Did she see me?' And then, suddenly, there she was. She'd seen it all—the clean round, the winning jump-off, everything. When she made her way through the crowd and gave me the greatest hug, I was just so happy! To me, that was the best horse show mom moment of all time."

Chapter 14

OLDER — AND WISER?

IT'S LATE AFTERNOON AND THE HUNTER

classes for the adult amateurs are about to begin. Show management knows better than to schedule these classes before lunch: The adults need time to digest their meals before jitters threaten to cause queasiness. Plus, the prospect of actually competing in the show ring takes some getting used to, sort of like wading toe-first into an icy pond. Observe, and you'll catch a glimpse of many of the amateurs as they transform, with trepidation, from civilian into equestrian. They don their breeches and boots, yet keep on their sunglasses, T-shirts, and straw hats. They slink, incognito, up to the back gate as if afraid to admit to the world—and to themselves—that yes, they are actually going to compete. They trudge up to the bulletin board at the back gate and stare at the course diagram. Their gaze is transfixed, almost meditative, as if hoping for some divine guidance. Attempting to channel fortitude from a sympathetic muse, they study the jumps and convince themselves that the oxer isn't really all that wide and the stone wall isn't truly as solid as it appears. Then they march, zombielike, back to the barn, temporarily steeled with courage, ready to button up the monogrammed choker and dust off the velvet hunt cap. "I am having fun" is the mantra chanted under their breath. "I am having fun."

There is a certain camaraderie among the adult amateurs that doesn't exist among the other divisions. The contentious junior medals and the rollicking jumper events resemble hand-to-hand combat in the battle for the blue. The adult amateur riders are a band of committed pacifists. There is a definite "We're all in this together" sort of vibe. It's similar to the nervous chitchat found in the waiting room of a dental clinic. Remarks such as "The last line seems to ride a little tight" serve only to fill the void before the gate swings open and the paddock steward, clipboard in hand, smiles that slightly demented dental hygienist grin and says, "Next."

Though there are rivalries in the adult amateur divisions—and certainly everyone covets the blue ribbon—most amateurs view showing as a passionate pastime. They are amateurs in the truest sense of the word in that they compete for the love of showing, not for the monetary gain or personal notoriety. Hence, the groans when a competitor chips into a line, and the gloved hands clasped to open mouths if someone's mount unseats his rider. As the class progresses, the collective temper of the participants rises and falls with any round that is particularly brilliant or shockingly calamitous. Among those yet to ride, the litany begins to swell. "I am having fun" is the self-affirmation. "I am having fun."

If there were service medals for brave equestrians, adult amateurs would surely win the bulk of them. The most coveted medal would be given for a bruised ego, which is the greatest challenge for most adult amateur riders. Most of these riders have careers far removed from the horse world. They are physicians, teachers, engineers, attorneys, and business entrepreneurs. There is also a smattering of show business celebrities. Such professionals have the respect of their coworkers, but they often must

struggle to gain the respect of their horses. At work these professionals give orders, write up employee evaluations, and make calculated decisions. In the show ring, it's the judge who is critiquing their performances. The amount of power one holds in the boardroom is nothing compared to the power emanating from the judge's booth. Did you successfully argue a case in court today? Big deal. Did you help teach a child to read? That's nice. Star in a film that grossed $100 million dollars? Wonderful. But now let's see if you can demonstrate two flying changes in a straight line, lope a perfect figure eight, or cleanly jump a course of fences in less than eighty seconds.

Beyond facing the challenges to their egos, adult amateurs also must confront the demon many of them try to outwit: age. Not only does age make for more sore muscles after a day of competing, and raise the concern that older bones aren't as solid as younger ones, but it can also sap one's strength. Many adult riders dismount after their classes and hand their reins to grooms, not because they shirk from manual labor, but because—dang it—they're tired! Some vintage competitors accept the inevitable effects of time and age with a mix of fatalism and humor.

When confronting the prospect of getting tossed off her high-spirited horse, Pam Mahony, a Kentucky-based horsewoman who's spent decades in the show ring, explains her mental approach thusly: "I stopped bouncing—when I got thrown—somewhere in my late thirties, which is when I broke my neck. In my forties, I was happy to land and roll, and not sustain too much damage. Now I just try not to make a crater that the paramedics have to dig me out of with pickaxes and shovels. It all just becomes relative."

At another time and in another place, Phoebe von Migula was a mover and shaker in the retail garment industry. But here and now, at the annual Saddlehorse Futurity, at the Los Angeles County Fair, she conjures up the image of Annie Oakley more than she does of Anne Klein. Sitting astride her 17-hand pinto saddlebred, Geronimo's Cadillac, von Migula exudes an easy confidence that can only come from decades spent in the saddle. It seems fitting that she wears a silky black blouse

dusted with rhinestones and is comfortably settled into her hand-tooled saddle with its silver swell and conchos. She is the doyenne of showmanship to which we all aspire. Her class is called to order, and she rides in first to lap the arena. Geronimo seems to know he is the group's best example of a western pleasure horse. He carries his amateur rider dutifully, his head high but not defiant. The communication between von Migula and the pinto is evident. Her reins are never taut, her posture never rigid. She is relaxed, the horse is calm, and their ride is pleasant to watch. And, she wins the class.

Back at the tack room, she supervises Geronimo's cooling out and offers him an armload of carrots, cooing, "What do good horses get? They get carrots!" While the pinto crunches his way to a frothy orange delight, von Migula sees to her own comfort. She readjusts her glasses, which are appropriately rose-tinted. Although von Migula won't reveal her true age, she does cheerfully admit to having spent more than half a century in the show ring (she began riding at age nine). She balances on one foot while she wriggles out of her show clothes and snuggles into a cotton pantsuit, all the while chatting with the enthusiasm of a teenager. "I have women friends my age who are very supportive of my showing. They're always asking me how I did at a show, what ribbons I won," says von Migula. "I think they realize that I still have a passionate interest in something." Inside the show

barn's ornate tack room hangs a large oval mirror before which von Migula stands, smoothing her platinum curls and fidgeting with her diamond earrings. Does she feel that her age has slowed her down, infringed on her ability to compete? She pauses for a moment and says, "I feel the same [as] I did twenty years ago. I work my horse myself six days a week. I just keep going."

Though it is a warm Southern California day at the end of summer, von Migula doesn't seem affected by the weather. The long blue ribbon she and Geronimo have just won seems to be the Fountain of Youth. Who could've guessed that the tonic of Eden that so many have sought over the centuries wasn't to be found in an exotic oasis or buried in a sacred tomb but embossed in gold lettering on the front of a blue streamer of ribbon? The words *First Place* seem to erase years. "Sometimes I catch a glimpse of myself in the mirror, and I think aloud, 'Who is that woman? Where did those wrinkles come from?'" says von Migula, echoing a sentiment shared by many adult riders. "Because that isn't what I envision myself looking like. I certainly don't feel old."

No, Phoebe, as long as you're in that silver saddle, you will forever be young at heart.

Chapter 15

OLD CAMPAIGNERS

IT'S EASY TO SPOT THE VETERAN SHOW HORSES.

They're the ones who don't shy as they pass the judge's booth or flick a suspicious ear toward the ring steward. These horses populate the classes for beginner riders, where they tolerate a child's loose heel thumping their sides and ignore unnecessary tugs on the rein. The equivalent of equine grandmas and grandpas, these four-legged baby-sitters faithfully serve as mounts to the next generation of blue ribbon winners. Study their wizened expressions during the lineup and you can almost hear them chatting amongst themselves:

So, who've you got today?

Oh, some kid in her first walk/trot classes. She's not too bad, but her legs could be tighter.

What about cookies? Does she give you cookies?

Nah. She's more of a carrot person.

When the class is pinned, regardless of the results, each horse invariably gets a hug around his neck from his diminutive rider. A young, cheeky face buried in the graying mane of a trusty horse is a reaffirming sight: youth acknowledging the benevolent wisdom of old age.

To keep these old campaigners fit and happy, they're provided with some tender love and care. Their aging joints, a tad stiffened by arthritis, take a few minutes to limber up. In preparation for their classes, they're either placed on the end of a longe line for a few laps or taken on a cruise around the show grounds. Their ears prick up in anticipation of performing, but rarely do they express enthusiasm beyond an animated toss of their head. The spirit is willing, but alas, the flesh is becoming weak. With their legs soothed with liniment rubs and coddled by layers of cotton and flannel, they look almost like war veterans as they stand in their stalls or rest at the trailers. But make no mistake about it. When their riders come to summon their help, bridle in one hand, obligatory carrot in the other, the competitive juices start to flow and the glint of youth seems to return to their eyes. As these older show horses are led to the back gate, a noticeable lilt to their step, it's not hard to imagine that they're thinking, *It's show time!*

In the jumping classes, these senior statesmen are known as packers because without much urging they will carry, or pack, their novice riders safely around a course. If blessed with good genes and given proper care, they can continue to compete into their late teens and early twenties. Along the way they acquire priceless experience, a tangible love for competition, and some quirky behavior.

B.J. Bullman lucked into a twenty-something Thoroughbred named Winter. After several years of dealing with a cantankerous mare who had no taste for the show ring, the chestnut gelding was a welcome change. Winter was a career show horse with a résumé that included stints as a dressage horse and a Grand Prix jumper. He was a perfect match to serve as mount and mentor to Bullman as she gained confidence in the novice hunter and equitation divisions. These days Winter often knows more about how to win a blue ribbon than his human pilot.

"Half the time I'm showing him, I feel like I'm having a conversation with him," says Bullman. "I'll turn toward a jump in a class, see my spot, and I can feel Winter thinking, *Are you sure that's what you want to do?* He'll let me know if he thinks I'm wrong because he'll flick his tail or grind his teeth on the bit, sort of like I'm this crazy person up here, but what the heck, he's got a job to do, so he grits his teeth and puts up with me." Like most opinionated, seasoned show horses, Winter has a limit to how gross of an error he'll accept. More than once Bullman has asked him to jump from an impossible takeoff and he's refused, costing her a ribbon. "In every instance, it was my fault. Thank goodness Winter knows more than me. He'll save me from myself. I'd rather have him refuse than ignore his instincts and land us both in the middle of a jump," she adds. "At his age, he's not a fool."

There was an attempt to retire Winter. He was pensioned out at a local ranch. He had his own paddock and a light workload of quiet hacks and trail rides. It was meant as a kind gesture, a thank you for two decades of dependable work, but he wasn't happy. He paced the fence and whinnied when other horses left for a day of showing. It was obvious that he envied the other horses as they climbed into the trailer for their road trip. When the adjacent ranch began hosting team penning and roping events, Winter would stand at the fence and watch, his ears pricked forward as the announcer called out the exhibitors' numbers. He hated being on the sidelines. That's how Bullman ended up with Winter. And he's happy now. When he enters the show ring, his cherry red coat glistens like that of a colt, and he carries himself like a racehorse going to the post. When he starts on course, Bullman barely has to cue him to canter. Winter knows his job. And that's just fine with Bullman.

Mares aren't famous for their loving, complacent dispositions, but an exception is a teenaged Appaloosa mare nicknamed Lacee. Not only is she a companion to her owner, Gail Simonz, but she has also been a favorite mount of several young riders. "Lacee was given to me when she was only seven months old. My friend owned her sire, and he wanted me to have one of the foals," says Simonz. "Now she's nearly fourteen, and it's safe to say that she knows I'm her mom. I keep her at home on my own half-acre. Every morning I get a welcome whinny from her when I step out the door."

Lacee is a strikingly beautiful Appy: a red roan the color of strawberry ice cream, with a brown-and-white spotted blanket across her hips. Her sparse mane and tail—though more lustrous than many of her kind—is a distinctive gray, the color of gun smoke. "Yeah, the kids are just really wowed by her color," admits Simonz. And a lot of kids have shown her. "She's a favorite mount for the lead liners. Five-year-old kids have won classes on her."

But the mare's main claim to fame is her versatility. She's the recipient of the Appaloosa Horse Club's Versatility Award given to horses who earn a Register of Merit in six different classes. That means that Lacee has accumulated a hefty number of points by winning events as varied as western,

English, trail, and gymkhana classes. Despite more than a decade of showing, the mare's attitude remains fresh. She seems to enjoy climbing into the trailer, whether the trip to the show is across the county or across the country. What's Simonz's secret to keeping the aging mare happy? "She gets a ton of R and R. She knows her job and how to do it. She doesn't need to be drilled. In between shows, she comes home and gets to roll in the dirt, tour the property, and just be a horse," adds Simonz. "I know my horse. If she gave me any clue that she didn't just love going into the show ring, I'd retire her."

Though the mare has won prestigious events from California to Oklahoma, there's one blue ribbon in particular that holds a tender place in Simonz's heart. Recently she loaned Lacee out to a charity show to benefit the local therapeutic riding club. A young disabled rider rode Lacee in both the trail class, where the quiet mare gingerly took the child over and through obstacles, and in the light-hearted egg and spoon race. In that class, the little girl had to balance an egg in a spoon for a longer time than others in the event. With her soft, easy gaits, Lacee won the class. "That blue ribbon meant the world to that little girl and her family. The smile on her face went on forever," says Simonz. "Despite all the ribbons Lacee has won over the years, I'll never forget that one. It was just so special, and my mare helped make it happen."

COMPETITORS HARBOR AMBIVALENT FEELINGS

toward horse show judges. On the one hand, the judge is the guru of the gathering and for this reason is regarded with reverence. As the absolute arbiter of success, the judge determines whether a performance is good or bad, who's a shining example of the show ring standard or a mediocre poser, and which horse is a blue ribbon winner or an also ran who merely fills the class. But the judge can also be viewed as an adversary.

As a rider, you must endeavor to impress the heck out of the judge or you'll never be noticed. Yet make a slight error and the judge is sure to draw a line of ink right through your number on the scorecard. Just like that, you're out of the ribbons. Add to this the element of subjectivity that clouds the decision-making process of most horse show events. Though judges must follow the guidelines for evaluating each class, there is usually some allowance for their personal preferences. Therefore, in a particularly tough class, where there's a virtual tie for first place, a judge with a penchant for silver horses might subconsciously be swayed to give the blue ribbon to the lone dapple gray. To those riders new to the world of showing, it may appear that judges as a group consistently give in to whims and vagaries of opinion, but rarely is that the case.

"I'm always aware that some riders have those kinds of feelings," says Robert McDonald, a respected hunter and jumper judge. "But I take my responsibilities seriously. It's easy for someone to watch just part of a class from the rail, and then complain about how the class was pinned. But they probably didn't watch every round or see the entire class. Perhaps they missed something I didn't," adds McDonald. "You know, let them sign their name to the cards and turn them in at the end of the day. They'll get a feeling for how much pressure a judge is under to do a good job."

This is not to claim that horse show judges aren't infallible. They do make mistakes. One story that made the rounds of the circuit, attaining legendary status, was an account of a prestigious hunter under saddle class. A well-known competitor, aboard her fancy Thoroughbred, had a few great passes in front of the judge, but her horse began to misbehave. Rather than disrupt the entire group, she discreetly excused herself the next time she circled past the gate. She watched the remainder of the class from the outside, leaning against the rail. She was both amused and astonished when her number was called out for fourth place.

But there's a flip side to the entire judge-competitor relationship that isn't heard quite so often. Judges sometimes have to take on the role of school principal or umpire, uncovering shenanigans that threaten the integrity of the sport. One judge told how he felt prompted to inspect the rather voluminous tail of a pony he was about to pin for first place in a conformation class. It turned out the tail was glued to the pony's hind leg in an effort to disguise a rather curby hock. A judge called to task by parents who'd circumvented the show steward was accused of marking their son off-pattern

in a western horsemanship class. Just as the fray was coming to a head, another parent stepped forward and offered as evidence videotape he'd been making of the entire class. It showed the boy had indeed made an error. Case closed.

When a judge establishes a reputation for being both fair and consistent in his decisions, he's understandably popular with competitors. Show managers take the hint: signing an admired judge to officiate ensures that classes will be filled. But the life of such esteemed judges is often far from glamorous. Take, for example, a couple of their encounters with long-distance traveling.

"I always try to carry on as much luggage as possible," admits Clay MacLeod, a renowned judge of quarter horses. He's ventured as far as Australia, Italy, and England to judge western performance events. "I always get a bad feeling when I have to check my luggage and I start walking one way at the airport and my bags are sent off in the other direction. I kind of learned my lesson the hard way," he laughs, recalling several occasions when his luggage made an uncharted detour. "Now I always dress in something I can judge in the next day if my luggage is, ah, 'misplaced.' That way I don't embarrass myself."

Hunter and equitation judge Andrea Meek's worst travel nightmare didn't involve lost luggage. Instead, she ended up bringing a suitcase full of the wrong wardrobe. "I'd signed a contract to judge a big show in Seattle, Washington," she recalls. The confirmed California beach girl called ahead to get a weather report. "They told me it was sunny and warm, so I brought just my typical skirt and blouse. I got there and it was freezing! Not only that but it also began to just rain torrents. Of course, the riders up there are used to that sort of environment, so they just put on their raingear and kept going. But me, I'm sitting outside in the back of this flatbed truck at a little table with an umbrella. Now mind you, it would've been a lovely patio umbrella, but it wasn't a rain umbrella. It leaked. Someone pitied me and brought me a big plastic trash bag with a hole cut in the top. I wore it like a poncho. That night the show steward drove me to a local department store. I bought myself the only weatherproof hat I could find: a fleece-lined, leather cap with earflaps. Now, if I wasn't a sight the next day. I sat out there wrapped up in a horse blanket wearing a cap that made me look like Elmer Fudd. Oh, so very chic!"

When they aren't battling airport demons, inclement weather, or disgruntled horse show parents, judges sincerely enjoy their profession. They've been exhibitors themselves. Many still compete. So not only do they sympathize with the riders they're scrutinizing but they also have a pretty good feel for how seriously some riders take the whole show experience.

Noted saddlebred judge Tom Sworm remarked how impressed he was with a certain horsewoman. Though an heiress to a considerable fortune, she schooled her own horses in the warm-up ring and rode in her classes not like a princess who thought she automatically deserved to win but like a gutsy, skilled competitor determined to earn her blue ribbons.

Then there are even some sentimental feelings that crop up. MacLeod related how he can't help but feel a little disappointed when a capable rider is prevented from winning a class because something just goes wrong. "I can't help but feel sorry for them," he admits. "Especially because I've been there myself, especially on a green horse. But as a judge, I'm bound by the rules. I just remind myself that if they're a true horseman, and a real competitor, they won't be kept down by one poor performance."

Meek has a soft spot for the real beginners in the walk/trot classes. She feels conflicted on those occasions when show managers ask her to pin the class, ranking them in order. That's great for the kid who takes the blue ribbon but not so much fun for the children left standing in the lineup empty handed. "I think they all deserve a ribbon, especially at the nonrated schooling shows. I think we need to encourage these kids. They're our next generation of riders. Sometimes they've had to overcome some real stage fright to get out there and compete. Plus, they have so much to remember at that point in their riding careers. It's a major effort posting on the correct diagonal, guiding their horse or pony, keeping their position, and staying out of traffic," explains Meek. To solve her moral dilemma, Meek maintains her own little stash of customized powder blue ribbons. She carries them around in her tote bag whenever she knows she's judging walk/trot classes. Each ribbon is stamped in gold with Judge's Special Award.

Chapter 17

AFTER HOURS

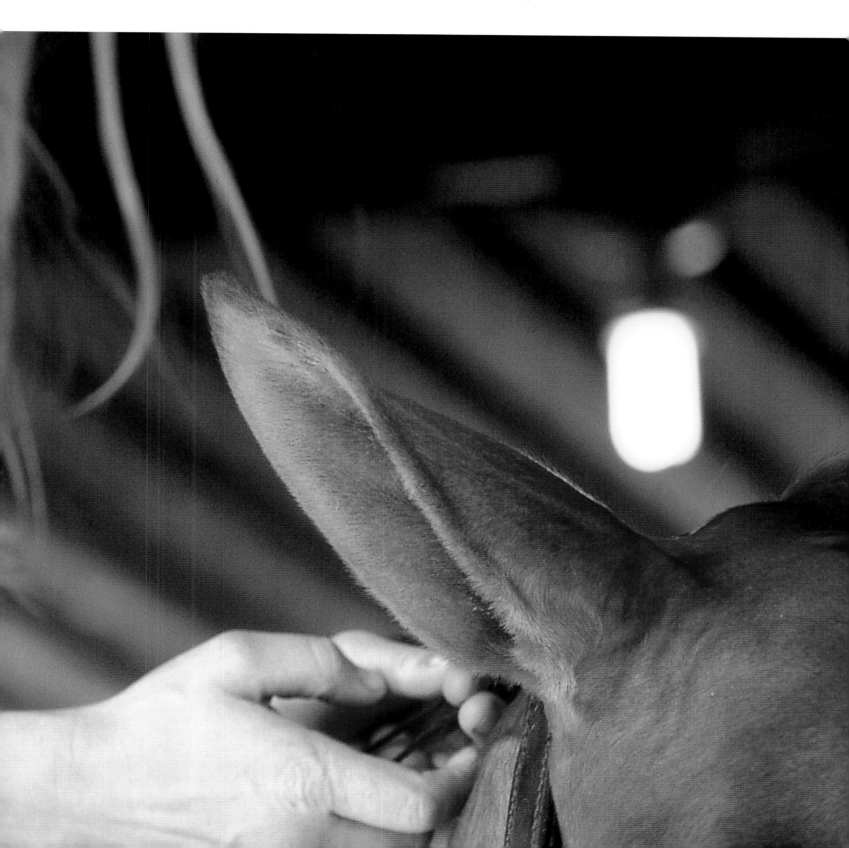

WITH THE LAST CLASS COMPLETED, THE JUDGE

leaves his score cards at the show office and heads for the motel. Since rules and ethics keep him from fraternizing with any exhibitors or their trainers, he'll probably order room service and watch television. But such seclusion is a welcome respite from the nonstop action of the day.

Back at the barns, riders break off into cliques. Some will venture to pizza parlors; others will choose more austere restaurants. The junior riders are notorious for strutting into the local Dairy Queen still wearing their show clothes (though a bit disheveled) almost daring the civilians to stare at them. Such is the brazen confidence of youth. Exhibitors on a budget or those who are just used to doing things their way, gather up armloads of tack and riding boots to cart back to their rooms for cleaning. Savvy hoteliers have learned to sacrifice a collection of ragged towels for such purposes.

About the only beings left behind are the horses themselves and the grooms. Once their charges have their legs wrapped and their bellies filled, the grooms will leave, too. The last people out are the ring crew—those who reset the jumps or replenish the arena's décor. Like stagehands performing a sound check or readjusting the lighting, they won't leave until the backdrop is ready for the next day's performance. Finally there is an audible hush as the show grounds settle down for the night.

Back in the stable area, the barns resemble a ghost town. The decorative drapes adorning each tack room are zipped shut. If you look closely, you'll discover a chain big enough to anchor a small boat secured to a padlock to lock the shrouded wooden door. Other tack rooms with doors removed to evoke more of a veranda motif harbor a surly watchdog behind each canvas curtain. Though he may be a genial hound riding shotgun in the golf cart seat by day, after dark he takes guard duty quite seriously. Thousands of dollars in leather goods, smelling faintly of turpentine and soap, are stored inside. Woe to anyone who ventures too closely after nightfall.

Though the dog may be on alert status most of the night, the horses are soon asleep. Most have their legs done up in square quilted pads and flannel wraps. This is done not only for support after a hard day's work but also because the stalls aren't quite roomy enough to allow a horse to really stretch out. The wraps help cushion the horse's legs if he bumps against a wooden partition, but the pajamas don't stop there. Show horse sleepwear runs the gamut from snoozing in the buff to being swathed in denier nylon from haunch to forelock. Even a horse's head and neck may be covered in a hood so that he begins to resemble an armored mount for a knight of King Arthur's round table. Ah, the indignities that come with being pampered.

Such valuable horses have their own guardian angels. At most large shows, a night watchman patrols the grounds. He might not be a confirmed horseman, but he has an affinity for the animals nonetheless. He knows not to shine his flashlight directly into their stalls, and he speaks calmly to settle any restless horses. Over the seasons he's captured many enterprising horses who have escaped for a midnight escapade. He has also summoned aid for an ailing show jumper and even thwarted a tack room burglary. But this night, as it is most other nights, the streets of the show grounds are peaceful. A horse might rumble the panels of his stall, his hooves bumping against plywood as he rolls in his fresh bedding, but otherwise the night is filled more with the scent of menthol liniment and molasses than it is with the sounds of activity. The watchman strolls to the end of the barn aisle,

glances at his watch, reaches for the clipboard hung on the wall by a half-twisted nail, and checks the box that confirms his post is secure.

Down one shedrow, a bright light beckons the night owl. Inside one of the show tents, where the horses are nestled in 10 x 10 canvas cubicles looking like prized eggs in a carton, a braider works intently. Her first name is Brenda, and she's already on her third horse, a testament to her work ethic and nimble fingers. She began her workday at midnight, and by dawn, she'll have earned more than $400 braiding the manes and plaiting the tails of show hunters. Like most professional braiders, Brenda follows the show circuit. If she's earnest enough, and builds up a list of prospective clientele, she can spend six weeks of the winter working the A-rated shows of Florida or California. Those are far more alluring gigs than the frigid venues of Connecticut or Washington.

The chestnut mare she's working on is dozing. The mare looks as if the crosstie chain is all that's supporting her head. Perhaps the radio's music is a lullaby to the mare, but the radio is Brenda's only companion. It doesn't seem to matter that the deejay rambles or the only music that can fight its way through the static is a forlorn collection of 1960s one-hit wonders. At least it breaks the solitude. Occasionally, due to condensation, a big drop of moisture forms on the ceiling of the tent and finally lets go, plunking onto Brenda's head and trickling down her nose. But she's not distracted. Her fingers, bound with strips of white medical tape to ward off blisters, dance across the horse's mane. For thirty miniature braids, the ritual is the same: wet hair with sponge, comb, part, braid, weave in the yarn, pull through, knot, and cut. When she reaches the midpoint of the mare's neck, she ties a small, red glass button to the braid. The mare's nickname is Ruby, and the red bauble is meant to be a subtle lucky charm. The judge probably won't notice the trinket. But it's Brenda's signature.

Like most professional braiders, Brenda was once a competitor. She learned to braid as a kid to earn extra bucks for entry fees. With her riding career behind her, a victim of finances and family constraints, she chooses to braid because it's a way for her to stay connected to the glamour and action of the horse show world. Brenda might not be performing, but like a Hollywood makeup artist, she's making certain her clients are ready for their close-ups. Show business, whether before a camera or before a judge, is an atmosphere that's difficult to walk away from.

Though sunrise is still more than an hour away, the predawn fog that lingers just above the ground has taken on a silvery glow. The mist has left its touch on everything left outside during the night. The ribbons hanging above the tack room threshold are a bit limp, and alfalfa stored discreetly at the end of the shedrow has taken on a bejeweled appearance. Stray stems that poke rigid fingers outside the bale are tipped with tiny beads of moisture. That's fine. Most horses appreciate a soft, dust-free breakfast. The initial sound that disturbs the show grounds' slumber is a rolling, growling rumble, distinctly automotive in its origins. It's the water truck. This huge, lumbering metallic beast conjures ambivalent reactions from competitors and horses. Though dust is indeed the enemy the water truck keeps at bay, the water truck does have its own flaws. First, it's a known fact that there are no new water trucks in existence. To everyone, they are pockmarked dinosaurs prone to breakdown, often requiring resuscitation before the show can resume. Their gears  grind in protest with each circuit of the arena. It's no wonder horses, particularly the green ones, dive in the opposite direction whenever one approaches. Second, they are forever hemorrhaging water. There seems to be no concept of just sprinkling the arena or the surrounding barn area. No, water gushes from the fountains fore and aft. By the time the sun has risen, the water truck has finished its tour of duty and limped back to its shed. But telltale puddles (tracks of the beast) are left behind. As the riders begin to arrive, you can overhear them asking, as they hop from one dry land bridge to another, "Did it rain last night?"

Chapter 18

THE RIBBON LADY

YOU CAN SENSE THE TENSION. THE SUPER-CHARGED

atmosphere during the class builds to a crescendo until the announcer instructs the riders to bring their horses down to a walk and line up in the center of the arena. There is no more squeaking of clean leather, no more pounding of oiled hooves on dusty ground. The moment of truth has arrived.

The competitors jockey for position, each trying to make sure the judge can see her number while the final tally is taken. With the last minute hustle completed, the expressions on the riders' faces are a study in concentration. Some are resigned to defeat, passing time until they can slouch back to the barn and lick their wounds. But most are forever hopeful. Though the English riders wear a mask of aloof concentration, their western counterparts often seem transfixed with a confident smile. Neither façade fools the experienced observer. The railbirds know what the riders are thinking: *Did the judge see my horse spook in the corner? Was my back straight enough? Was my trot too slow, my canter too fast?*

Regardless of a rider's riding discipline, the experience in the line-up is the same: her shirt is stuck to her skin from sweat because of nerves, her hat is creasing her brow, and, deep within her boots, her feet have lost all sensation. If only she didn't have to hold her rigid posture any longer. Yet she maintains her grip on the reins and nudges her horse with her heel if he threatens to move. She strains her ears, trying to decipher the string of numbers the judge is whispering to the announcer over his walkie-talkie. And then, the arena gate opens and in strolls the ribbon lady, her arms overflowing with colored satin streamers and one hand gingerly balancing the first place prize like a treasured artifact.

At the large shows, which are often events benefiting a local charity, the ribbon lady is usually a nattily attired volunteer who may be only vaguely acquainted with horse show protocol. Though the ribbons are stacked in order, you can still hear the ribbon lady nervously muttering under her breath, "Blue, red, yellow, white, pink," as she tentatively takes her place in front of the battalion of horses. Regardless of the ribbon lady's trepidation, the competitors afford her the same level of homage given Venus as she emerged from the sea— she comes bearing wondrous gifts.

Something special is missing from shows that have dispensed with ribbon ladies. Maybe expediency or a lack of willing subjects has caused the decline. Unless an enthusiastic child is handy, ribbons often get relegated to a wire coat hanger at the back gate, casually plucked off its rack. Placements in the competition are announced—there are a few whoops and hollers—but that's it for the ceremony. It's just so much grander when someone actually hands out the awards.

Bobbie Werner-Hausen has been a horse show ribbon lady for nearly eight years. As an active member in the Arabian Horse Association of Southern California, she's taken it upon herself to be the Madame of Ceremonies at several large competitions. To Werner-Hausen, it's a labor of love. Her only compensation is free lodging, but she gains a personal reward by adding elegance and panache

to a rider's win photo. As a competitor herself, she recalls winning an important class only to have the ribbon presenter saunter into the arena wearing jeans and a sweatshirt. "I looked nice, my horse looked beautiful, but the gal presenting the awards, well, she detracted from the whole picture. I didn't buy the photograph, and I want our exhibitors to buy their pictures. It's not only a memento, but many of them will also be used in national advertisements," she adds proudly.

To help set the stage for a photogenic moment, Werner-Hausen travels with a vast enough wardrobe to supply her with three changes of clothes per day: one outfit for the morning events, another for after lunch, and a special number for the more formal evening classes. When she's not changing clothes, she's hustling back and forth from horse show office to trophy room readying the prizes for the upcoming classes. "I have nice dress shoes I wear when I trudge into the arena so my whole outfit looks put together," says Werner-Hausen. "But then I slip my tennis shoes back on." More than once her dressy shoes have been caught beneath the foot of an impatient or camera-shy horse. No doubt she just kept smiling for the picture. Werner-Hausen's typical show day runs from early morning until about midnight. But such things as hectic schedules don't dampen the spirit of a true ribbon lady. "I've had people see me at shows or at other horse functions and say, 'I know who you are. I recognize you from my win photos!' That's kind of nice. Plus, I can't help but really feel excited for the kids who are winning their first championship, or the amateur adults. They put so much effort and time into their riding and often have to make so many sacrifices to show. They just get so excited when I drape that ribbon around their horse's neck."

I crossed paths with my own special ribbon lady many years ago. My trainer had this seemingly innocuous plan to combine a horse show with a vacation. So the entire barn—about a dozen horses, all of us young riders, and our respective horse show moms and dads—caravanned to the San Francisco bay area. After several days of ceaseless tourist stops and lackluster show ring performances, some of us were ready to hitchhike home. As the self-appointed ringleader of the junior equitation riders, I decided to jump start the whole awful experience. To bolster my chances for a ribbon in my upcoming equitation class, I pulled out my horse for an extended warm-up session. I wrenched the stirrups off my saddle and rode without irons for half an hour. My thighs were burning and blood oozed from rub marks on the insides of my knees, staining my breeches. But I pressed on. I had my

mercurial gelding, Bubbles, so focused on me that he hardly noticed when twenty more horses and riders joined us, forming a cauldron of hooves and hunt coats in the schooling ring.

When the class began, I rode as if the reputation of the barn rested on my performance. If Bubbles raised his head to study some distraction in the distance, I squeezed my aching legs to send him back to the bit. If I felt myself start to slump from exhaustion, I found the strength to pull my shoulders back. When the class was over and we lined up, it seemed like the group of riders stretched from one end of the turf arena to the other. I spied my barn mates along the picket fence rail. They looked like a pack of starving dogs, begging for a bone. But had I been good enough?

Here came the ribbon lady wearing a stretchy polyester blouse, complete with puffy sleeves and a bright paisley print. A pair of cat-eye sunglasses—ostentatious even for that era—dominated her face. Reflected in her sunglasses was the glow of a huge silver platter, which held the long, azure ribbon. When my name was announced as the winner, I lost all composure. I was overcome with a mixture of relief, vindication, and utter joy. Apparently it was infectious, because the ribbon lady's eyes became teary behind her Cat Woman glasses. After the win photo was snapped, she reached up and awkwardly hugged me, her plastic earring bouncing off my leather glove, her sleeve becoming sullied with horse sweat. Even now, when I look at that old black-and-white photograph, sooty with age, I relive that moment with my ribbon lady. Still flush with youth, it was a time when I began to understand there were indeed rewards for perseverance.

Chapter 19

A Test of Character

THERE ARE MANY WAYS TO BE A BLUE RIBBON WINNER.

There is the gracious winner, who smiles demurely, pats her horse, and all but curtsies before accepting the prize. Then there is the triumphant winner. Flush with the vigor of victory, an arm is thrust in the air, pumping along with an exclamation of, "Yes!" The apologetic winner seems embarrassed to pick up the blue, grasping it with a sheepish grin. Surprised winners seem affected by amnesia, unaware that they truly were the best in their class. They're so transfixed in the lineup that they don't seem to hear their number called. When someone finally yells from the rail, "Hey, Betsy, that's you," it's almost as if the rider was snapped back to reality from a hypnotic trance. Open your eyes now. You've won a blue ribbon.

There aren't many ways to be a loser. In fact, it seems there are only two: the good loser and the sore loser. The good loser has gained a perspective on horse shows. Today the blue evades her. Next month she could be champion. Call it recognizing the ebb and flow of positive and negative outcomes—a Zen approach to equestrianism—but there is an inner peace that comes with accepting the inevitable disappointments that arise when a human is paired up with a horse. Sometimes the horse just won't cooperate. Or a minor error cost the blue. A missed lead change, a rolled jump rail, or a spook in the corner can mean going back to the barn empty-handed. But above all else, the good loser accepts

that sometimes she is just plain outridden: Another competitor was more accurate or more graceful. Another horse was simply more stylish or more athletic. The good loser accepts defeat as a fact of showing. Sure, she's disappointed. But she saves her tears for that quiet place in the back corner of the tack room when no one's around, when only the horses, noses pressed to the walls, can hear the sobs. If the good loser ever vents, letting loose with recriminations about the judge's intellectual capabilities, it is only before an audience of horses and dogs. A good loser never rants in public.

In defiant contrast, the sore loser has a list of reasons why the blue ribbon eluded her. The judge doesn't like her, her horse, or her trainer. The striding between the jumps was off. The footing in the arena was bad. Her horse didn't like the venue. All that's missing from the diatribe of excuses is a mournful violinist in the background. Once in a while an innocent bystander gets caught in the crossfire. The secretary in the show office, the show photographer, the water truck driver—they're all liable to be lambasted for simply occupying space within the same realm of existence that the sore loser perceives as some sort of purgatory. If a horse show—once it's distilled down to its basic elements—is an evaluation of character, the sore loser fails the test.

Whether a rider is a good or bad loser, the unknowns, which tend to make anxiety levels rise before a big show, test a rider's true character. As the day approaches, riders polish their boots, tuck their outfits into their zippered bags, and clean their tack. Riders almost hate to admit it but they have already ridden their horsemanship pattern a hundred times over in their minds, and by the way, they were perfect. In their daydreams, even the judge applauds their performances. But a rider cannot compete at a horse show without the most integral part: the horse himself. That's why many fantasies are ruined when an otherwise sound horse comes up sore right before a competition. Oh, if

only a horse could converse, rather than playing a game of charades where you stand before the animal and observe his symptoms by blurting out guesses like, "I think it's the right hock." Or, if only the horse could respond, "I was fine until I tripped slightly coming out of my stall and felt a pull in my stifle. Really, it doesn't feel like much of anything. I'm sure I'll be fine tomorrow. In the meantime, got any carrots?" But horses have yet to provide us with a universal translator. So while a rider is in a state of hysteria wondering whether she'll make it into the show ring next weekend, her vet arrives on the scene with the aplomb of Sir Galahad. Surely, he will save her and her plans!

Modern veterinarians have a number of medications and therapies at their disposal to soothe a sport horse who has pulled up lame. Despite this medical bag of marvels, the vast majority of practitioners put the welfare of their patients first. It's unethical to risk the future of an equine athlete just for the sake of some nonrefundable entry fees. Besides, the rules governing horse shows place strict controls over which medications can be given and in what quantities. Designated testers wander the show grounds, choosing horses at random to check for forbidden substance by drawing blood or urine samples. In keeping with human nature, there is a temptation to use every measure to eek out one more round of jumps, one more duel with a steer, or one more pass by the judge's booth. To say that there are not people in the show world who lurk just outside the rules and squeal about selective enforcement when they're caught is to deny the darker side of showing. Those folks have forgotten that part of horsemanship is sportsmanship. They lack compassion for their horses—and they lack character.

Horse shows teach us lessons about life. How we respond to success and failure in the show ring teaches us about ourselves. First, if you fall off, no matter how dusty your jacket or how scuffed your boots, if you're physically uninjured, climb back on. Neither life nor horse shows are for the fainthearted. Second, have realistic expectations. A well-respected judge once advised exhibitors to "show against your peers." In other words, don't drag your backyard crossbred to a national horse show and expect to win blue ribbons against blue-blooded horses. Like it or not,

there's a hierarchy in much of life. Find where you fit, discover your own little pond, and go swimming there. Finally, be brave and rise to the occasion. Life presents adversity every day. Though everyone should know her limitations, there should also be room for facing personal challenges. Otherwise we might as well cuddle up in a corner.

"I don't like to read anyone's stories about overcoming fear," says Constance Martin, an amateur rider who's returned to jumping competition after a long hiatus. She shies away from trading war stories with riders who've suffered bad falls and lived to ride again. Such topics are taboo, lest they creep into her consciousness and take up residence. "Sometimes I can just feel that knot in my gut when I know the jumps are being raised," she admits, revealing that her ears are quite keen to that unmistakable metallic sound of a steel pin and jump cup being repositioned on a standard. "But I've learned to trust my horse and my trainer." So she grits her teeth, quells her fears, and gallops down to the jump, all the while knowing that if she ever hopes of winning a blue ribbon, she must conquer all self-doubts about her abilities.

Being brave doesn't come naturally. It's a character trait that must be developed. And one of the best places to learn it is on the back of a show horse.

Chapter 20

ON THE ROAD—AGAIN

HORSE SHOW FOLKS ARE A PORTABLE GROUP.

To outsiders we must surely seem like a clan of nomads wandering the countryside in search of that next oasis, which fortune tells us is an oval arena, a shaded grandstand, a judge, and an assortment of ribbons. Whether it's a one-day show or a weeklong marathon, the journey begins with the same ritual: packing the tack trunk, tossing hay into the bed of the pickup, and hitching up the horse trailer. Those of us who are mildly neurotic keep our show gear locked and loaded in our tack trunks and trailers so we'll be ready to compete at a moment's notice. The more nonchalant types, perhaps in a state of denial, wait until the last moment and heave the show equipment onto the rig at about the same time the horses are ambling up the ramp. Perhaps the ambivalence is rooted in the knowledge that everything put on the truck eventually must be unloaded at the show grounds, put to use, and then torn down and reloaded for the trip home. While multiday shows require the greatest quantity of items, owing to the feed supplies alone, the one-day shows demand the most ingenuity since they rarely conclude as scheduled.

Invariably there's a standard notation found at the bottom of the premium that reads, "Good food will be served all day." It is viewed with a mere wink and a nod, given about the same credence as the promise, "Plenty of shade." To combat these "promises," the experienced exhibitor carts along a cooler full of homemade goodies. It's not unusual for tailgate parties to become the central focus of afternoon activities. The battle cry becomes, "To heck with the equitation classes, the people from Carousel Farm brought shrimp salad!"

Thwarting the afternoon sun becomes the second priority. The favored defense is an item more closely related to garden parties: the awning. This lightweight sunscreen consists of nothing more than an armload of plastic poles and a canvas cloth that slips over the frame. Thanks to the evolutionary process, the portable awning is now so simple to set up that a pair of trained monkeys could whip the thing together in a few minutes. Well, allegedly.

My sister, cousin, and I traveled a local show circuit one summer. As a gift, we received a striped awning neatly tucked inside its coordinating striped canvas bag. We tossed it into the tack compartment of the horse trailer and eagerly anticipated the day when we could unfurl it beside our trailer at a show and lounge in comfort between classes.

The debut of the unfurling came at a particularly hot and arid show. I saddled up and left for my first class, leaving my sister and cousin behind, the two of them ominously scratching their heads and peering over the sheet of directions, which they insisted were written in unfamiliar lingo. I finished both rounds of hunters and strolled back to the trailer only to find what looked like a pile of long plastic matchsticks and a decidedly unfurled awning. When I mocked their efforts, I was handed one of the tent stakes and instructed to "Go ahead. Try driving it into the ground." I grabbed the nearest blunt object, a heavy wooden boot jack, and whacked the end of the stake. My hand stung. Not only had I not made a dent in the earth but the plastic had also cracked! It was then I declared I'd discovered a design flaw. How could anyone be expected to drive a plastic stake, pointed or not, into the granitelike footing of the typical horse show parking lot?

By now our fellow exhibitors were intrigued. We didn't have to ask for assistance. Riders—still in their show clothes—wandered over to take up the challenge. Classes continued in the arenas. Ribbons were won. But no one cared. They were consumed with this construction project. An hour went by. More than once there was an attempt to decipher the incoherent instructions. Then there'd be a resounding curse, a crumbling of paper, and they'd be tossed aside. The awning itself began to resemble a beaten, abused beast. It lay heaved in the corner, near the obtusely angled "roof" that had fallen down. I finally had to tramp back to the show arena for my flat classes, leaving the spectacle behind me.

When I returned, it was to urge my sister and cousin to get ready for their events. I wholly expected to pull off my boots and relax under the awning, which surely had been erected. But once again, no

such luck. The remains of the awning were left kicked and scattered in a denigrated pile of plastic and canvas. One onlooker, an unfamiliar horse show mom, greeted my look of disbelief with a broad smile. "Oh, don't be upset," she said warmly. "Watching the entire fiasco was far more entertaining than the horse show."

If the impediments at the show grounds don't deter a penchant for traveling, then the risks of hauling horses and ponies on the freeways of America surely will. "The scariest part is breaking down," said Appaloosa trainer Kristin Keeler. "I'm usually hauling six horses, including a stallion and some mares. What am I supposed to do? Go for help? How? Ride one horse and lead the other five?" Keeler's journeys on the Appaloosa show circuit have taken her and her gooseneck, six-horse trailer across Texas, Oklahoma, California, and Montana. And that was just in one month. "I think my biggest frustration is stopping for meals. I'm always so conflicted," she says. "Don't even ask how I maneuver this huge rig into a parking lot. It's an art. I usually send someone in to get me a hamburger because I don't want to leave the rig unattended. Invariably, when I do decide, 'Ah, it'd be nice to wash my hands and face and sit inside,' I come back out to the parking lot and find that we're now boxed in between a minivan and a Fiat with no hopes of escaping."

Since horse show folks spend so much time on the road, it's understandable that they take pride in their hauling vehicles, often christening them with vanity license plates bearing cryptic equestrian messages. The pickup trucks are shiny, their chrome wheels glistening, but peer inside the cabs and immediately they're identified as belonging to horse show entrants. The seats are upholstered with dog hair and the floor mats are littered with a sprinkling of alfalfa leaves and wrappers from the local taco joint.

The decorated tack rooms at horse shows are awarded more sacred status. They appear to be spawned from the imagination of an overactive interior decorator. These are not merely vacant extra stalls used to house equipment for the week. In an unwinnable game of one-upmanship, stables seem to compete for who can amass the most ostentatious assortment of chrome-lidded tack trunks, plaid wool horse blankets, and leather halters. Entering one of these tack rooms is like stepping into a sanctuary. No one talks much. No one touches anything, either. Not the polished brass candlesticks, not the commissioned artwork, not the bowl of fresh fruit serving stoically as the centerpiece on the linen-clad table. Heaven forbid that someone should plop their fanny down in one of the embroidered director's chairs without first patting their derriere free of dust.

It is a harmless enterprise, decorating one's tack room to the hilt. It certainly keeps the canvas manufacturers in business. But pity the poor grooms, who have to unpack, set up, and then tear down the whole estate, only to repeat the process the next month or so, when the stable goes on the road again.

Each weekend, countless riders in their vans and trailers caravan across highways shuttling their cargo from home to horse show. And, each weekend, the pageantry unfolds anew as another show begins. It is an atmosphere brimming with esthetic beauty, kinetic energy, and barely constrained emotions. Stainless steel bits and stirrups glisten in the morning sunlight. The crisp air is tinged with the scent of coat polish while grooms gather like worker bees around a horse. Who will win a blue ribbon today? And who will be left to ponder just what went wrong?

Whether it's a child aboard a spiteful pony, a world-class rider vying for a spot on an international team, or a cowgirl bringing her quarter horse to a sliding stop, the mission is the same: to ride for the blue. Though eventually the blue ribbons may fade to a nondescript shade of violet and become frayed around the edges, the memories a rider recalls about a day spent on the back of a beloved horse competing among friends remain evergreen.

Glossary

aids: cues used to communicate with a horse

also ran: a horse or rider that fails to win a ribbon

bradoon: a small bit used in tandem with a larger curb bit; a part of a dressage full bridle

bridle: head gear on a horse that includes the bit and reins

bombproof: an extremely quiet, totally trustworthy horse

bloodstock agent: someone who brokers pedigreed horses; a dealer for purebred horses

canter: a three-beat gait that has a rocking horse motion; it is smoother and slower than the gallop

caulks: small bumps or cleats placed on horse shoes to add traction

cayuse: an old western term for feral horse of undetermined bloodlines

chip: an awkward short step the horse adds right before he takes off for a jump in jumping competition

circuit: a series of related horse shows, usually offering year-end championships

cluck: the distinctive sound a rider makes with her mouth to encourage her horse

conchos: decorative silver buttons

diagonals: the movement in which a horse's legs move in diagonal pairs. English riders post (rise out of the saddle) at the trot on the correct diagonal, meaning they're in rhythm with the rising of the horse's outside shoulder.

equitation: the act or art of riding on horseback. In equitation classes, the rider's position and control of her mount is scrutinized.

flatwork: riding skills that focus on perfecting the basic gaits and the horse's balance; no jumping is included

flying change: a change of leading leg with a skipping motion performed while the horse continues to canter or lope

futurity: special classes offering prize money for the best young horse

Grand Prix: high levels of competition for both jumpers and dressage horses; generally equal to international standards

groundperson: a riding assistant who coaches in the warm-up ring; may also set practice jumps

gymkhana: timed events (also called games) such as barrel racing and pole bending, usually performed under western tack

hack: an English riding term for horse show classes not held over jumps. It is also a common name for the hunter under saddle class and used to describe pleasure riding.

hackamore: a bitless bridle that works by applying pressure on a horse's nose and jaw

high point: a show or circuit award given to the horse and/or rider accumulating the most points for ribbons won

irons: stainless steel stirrups found on English saddles

jump-off: a shortened course of jumps ridden against the clock to break a tie for first place

kimberwicke: a type of English bit that often features a solid mouthpiece

latigo: the long leather strap that connects and adjusts a cinch to a western saddle

lead(s): a position a horse must take during the canter or lope where one front leg leads the stride, striking the ground farther ahead of the other front leg and the opposite rear leg

lead line: a horse show class in which young children are paraded at a walk around the show ring, their horses and ponies led by an adult

lead rope: a long piece of braided rope that attaches to a horse's halter so the handler can guide the horse, similar to a dog's leash

longe: to exercise a fresh horse by placing him on the end of a long rope and allowing him to trot and gallop in a circle

lope: the western term for canter

martingale: an item of tack used to help lower or set the horse's head

medal class: a prestigious equitation class in which the judge may ask for additional tests of a rider's skill

muck: to clean a stall

off-pattern: straying from the judge's prescribed course; also called off course

oxer: a type of jump consisting of two vertical fences set close together, one behind the other, with the height closely matching the depth

Pelham: an English bit of moderate severity with a solid mouthpiece

piaffe: a difficult movement primarily seen in the upper levels of dressage wherein the horse appears to trot in place

pin: the order in which the judge places the contestants in a class

premium: the flyer or booklet for a horse show that lists the classes and other pertinent information

rack: an energetic specialized gait of the American saddlebred

railbird: a horse show spectator who typically leans against the arena railing to support a competitor

rated show: a competition sanctioned or recognized by a governing riding association that awards points or championships to winners. "A" rated shows award the most prize money and attract the stiffest competition.

rating: regulating a horse's approach to a jump; a western horse's gate

riata: a short, coiled rope; a small lariat

rowels: revolving disks with sharp marginal points at the end of a spur

romal: the long leather thong attached to a particular style of western reins

school: to train or reprimand a horse

school horse: a horse primarily used by a riding school as a lesson mount

scope: the measure of a horse's ability to jump across a wide fence

shedrow: barn aisle area in front of a horse's stall

snaffle: the most common type of English bit; it is generally mild and has a jointed mouthpiece

steward: a horse show official responsible for enforcing rules and protocol

studs: male horses used for breeding; caulks applied to horse shoes

stud chain: a short brass or stainless steel chain attached to a lead rope to better control a headstrong horse

swell: the prominent ridge on the front of a western saddle

tempi changes: changes of lead done every few strides in upper level dressage

turn-out: a presentation of a horse's and/or rider's appearance before a judge

tobiano: a coat pattern found in paint or pinto horses

USAEquestrian: a national riding association that provides rules and officials for its sanctioned shows in America (formerly the American Horse Shows Association)

vertical: a jump composed of a single element such as a gate or panel

warmblood: a variety of horse breeds, all of whom descended from sturdy native European stock (cold blood) that were crossed with the more refined Thoroughbred (hot blood). As a group, warmbloods are desired for jumping and dressage due to their hefty size, expressive gaits, and dependable temperament.